THE EXAMINATION OF ANIMALS
FOR SOUNDNESS

The Examination of Animals for Soundness

By

R. H. SMYTHE,
M.R.C.V.S.

1959

LONDON

CROSBY LOCKWOOD & SON LTD
26, OLD BROMPTON ROAD, S.W.7.

*Printed in Great Britain by Richard Clay and Company, Ltd.,
Bungay, Suffolk*

PREFACE

DURING the past twenty years the pattern of veterinary practice has changed, and whereas it was the custom to employ the veterinary surgeon whenever the question of horse purchase arose, his services have become less in demand for this purpose owing to the decline in the number of horses. He is called in much more often than previously, however, to examine animals of other species, and according to the locality in which he practises and the clients who employ him, he may be asked, nowadays, to examine animals of many kinds, ranging from elephants and camels down to hamsters and budgerigars.

Of late, the number of ponies, riding horses, and show jumpers has once more increased, and as their market value has soared to great heights, the practitioner is again being called in with great regularity to decide upon their soundness before they change hands. In addition, he is employed to examine farm stock for private buyers, or in connection with auction sales, as well as various animals, including a large number of valuable pedigree dogs, for the purpose of export.

His services are also required in connection with the examination of horses in sale yards and on race-courses, and to decide whether they are sound in the show ring.

He may be appointed to examine racing greyhounds for the various tracks, monkeys and other animals used for laboratory purposes, horses and ponies owned by riding schools, as well as zoological specimens of all kinds. It is also likely that before long the veterinary surgeon will be employed to examine all animals intended for human consumption prior to their slaughter.

v

The increase in the value of pedigree stock casts a greater responsibility on the veterinary surgeon, and the present-day tendency of the animal-buying public to rush into litigation on the slightest provocation does not make his position any easier. It is only proper that the veterinary surgeon should be fully qualified to examine a valuable horse or other animal and decide the question of its soundness.

Unfortunately, the rapid depletion in the horse population which occurred when mechanical transport supplanted them in the fields as well as on the roads gave rise to the belief, even in veterinary circles, that the horse would shortly remain with us only as a specimen in a museum or zoological garden. In consequence, the training of the veterinary student, which hitherto had centred around equine soundness, became devoted more and more to other animals, so that the study of the horse tended in some teaching centres to be regarded as of less importance than it had ever been. In addition, the students themselves had become more mechanically minded, and the intricacies of the internal-combustion engine held a greater place in their thoughts than did the dynamics of the horse.

In the course of time youth deserted the stable and congregated in the garage, and so failed to make the contact with horses which had previously afforded delight, until eventually young men began to consider the horse as being a little beneath their notice when regarded as a medium of transport. Fortunately, their sisters did not always share their views.

In consequence, now that the horse has again come into the picture, the recent graduate so often approaches this animal with a vague misgiving. The purpose of this book is to restore in some degree the technique which in former years earned the profession the esteem of the horse-loving public. It is hoped that the volume may be of service to the younger members of the profession and to all who have lost touch with the horse in these mechanised times, and that it will help them to carry out the examination of animals for soundness with peace of mind engendered by a greater feeling of confidence.

I should like to take this opportunity of expressing my thanks to Mr. J. K. Bateman, B.Sc., M.R.C.V.S., and Miss Margaret Bentley, M.R.C.V.S., to whom I am indebted for their respective contributions (Chapters 6, 7) "The Examination of the Greyhound", and "The Examination of the Cat".

CONTENTS

Chapter One

THE EXAMINATION OF THE HORSE

HORSES are examined for soundness for a variety of reasons. They may be stallions purchased for stud or for racing with a view to their being placed at stud at a later date, or they may be examined for purpose of registration under the Horse Breeding Acts of 1918 and 1948.

Mares may be acquired to ride or drive, race or jump, or in order that they may produce foals.

The animals submitted for examination will vary in age; they may be recently born foals or aged horses destined for slaughter; they may be yearlings of great value to be trained as race-horses, or they may be ponies kept at a riding establishment.

Horses exist in a variety of types and may be used for a number of purposes. It is for this reason that distinct breeds have been developed so that animals can be found capable of any particular work in which horses are commonly employed. On the other hand, horses of mixed breed are used in trade vehicles and are frequently very suitable as hunters and for hacking and driving. A good vanner, for instance, will possess sufficient weight to be able to pull a load and yet be sufficiently active to trot with it on level ground.

Horses are frequently examined in connection with auction sales. They may comprise Thoroughbred stock suitable for racing or breeding; they may be foals, yearlings or two-year-olds, or they may be race-horses which have won valuable races. Sales of hunters are also held frequently, either at the end of the beginning of a season, sometimes at hunt stables, at other times at repositories.

Although the present increase in the number of horses is mainly among animals of the types required for gymkhanas, exhibitions, hunting and show-jumping, and more particularly among ponies and light horses ridden by children and young people, the veterinary surgeon may also be asked to examine cobs, hacks, and harness horses by private buyers or to give his opinion as to whether an animal which is not completely sound is likely to be found capable of fulfilling the requirements of the prospective purchaser.

Sometimes an examination is not a complete one but made in order to decide whether a horse is sound in wind, eyes or both, or only to determine its correct height. In the latter case the veterinary surgeon may be acting privately, or as an official examiner, or as a referee in a case in which the height of an animal has been disputed.

Thoroughbreds come into a category almost their own. The examination of racing stock may be carried out for a private owner or intending purchaser, in connection with a sale of stock or upon a race-course during a meeting. It may be the duty of the veterinary surgeon to examine horses before or after a race, even during the course of one in case of accident, or he may be required to take samples of saliva or other materials whenever a suspicion of doping arises. He may also be asked to express an opinion as to whether a horse has been submitted to any treatment, or in any way interfered with, which may influence the chances of its winning or losing a race.

The integrity of the veterinary surgeon has become a by-word, and in connection with soundness and its determination his opinion is regarded by the public as irreproachable.

The abbreviation "vet" has been adopted in verb form to signify an honest and careful consideration of a project. It is therefore imperative that the veterinary surgeon shall never express any opinion concerning the soundness or otherwise of any animal before he has considered very carefully every aspect of the particular case. It is equally necessary that his knowledge shall be adequate in order that the opinion he expresses will be substantially correct.

Over the years a great deal of discussion has centred around the definition of the word "soundness" as it is applied to the horse. It must be accepted that few horses, and for that matter few animals of any other species bred and reared in conditions of domestication, can be described as completely sound.

But there are variations in degrees of unsoundness, just as there are differences in the nature of the defects which animals exhibit. Some are trivial, and although they may be regarded merely as eyesores, cause little interference with the physical capability of the animal and develop no tendency to do so. Others constitute severe handicaps to the usefulness of the horse, although in some cases there may later be partial or complete recovery of usefulness or, on the other hand, the unsoundness may remain permanent and even become more severe with the passage of time, particularly if the animal is compelled to continue working.

Many unsoundnesses are congenital. They may be recognisable soon after birth, or it may be an undesirable type of conformation which is transmitted. The animal thus endowed is incapable of withstanding the stress of its work and environment and develops obvious unsoundness as the result, usually quite early in life.

Then, too, there are the acquired blemishes which are associated with certain types of work, which may never seriously interfere for long periods with the ability of the animal to perform its duties. Such blemishes may be regarded as

fair wear and tear, to be expected in a considerable proportion of horses thus engaged.

It would be quite unusual if a veterinary surgeon, asked to
examine a hunter which had performed regularly for three or
four seasons, found himself unable to detect a blemish or unsoundness of any description. It would therefore be quite
misleading to assert that the majority of working horses, even
when of high value, were completely sound, just as it would
be to label every animal possessing some minor blemish
as unsound.

From the above it will be realised that any definition of
soundness, as applied to the horse, must entail a little elasticity, but there must be a limit to this, and it should not be
permissible to stretch its meaning beyond certain well-defined
boundaries.

It is now generally accepted that an unsoundness is any
defect likely to interfere with the usefulness of the animal
in the performance of any work at which it may be reasonably
employed.

The legal definition of soundness is based on the judgement
of Baron Park (1842), who declared: "The rule as to soundness is that if at the time of sale the horse has any disease
which actually does diminish the natural usefulness of the
animal so as to make him less capable of work of any description, or which in its ordinary progress will diminish the
natural usefulness of the animal, or if the horse has either
from disease or accident undergone any alteration of structure that either actually does at the time or in its ordinary
effects will diminish the natural usefulness of the horse, such
a horse is unsound."

In spite of this definition there are, however, many conditions met with in horses which must be classed as unsoundness whenever encountered, although it is quite likely
that an animal possessing certain of these defects might
be able to perform normal work throughout its lifetime

without exhibiting any lack of usefulness attributable to them.

Among the defects which must always be recorded as producing unsoundness may be included:

(*a*) Any interference with respiration such as may be caused by chronic cough, emphysema of the lungs (broken wind) and any tendency, however slight, to "make a noise". This includes any degree of whistling or roaring but not those noises produced voluntarily, such as high-blowing or snorting, unless these are associated with over-fatness and inability to take active exercise.

(*b*) Defects of the teeth which may interfere with grazing or mastication. These include overshot and undershot mouths, as well as defects of the cheek teeth or incisors.

(*c*) Certain faults and vices such as "shivering", stringhalt, weaving, crib-biting, and windsucking.

(*d*) Blindness (partial or complete) and deafness.

(*e*) Any spinal abnormality or any nervous disorder involving the loss of the full use of muscles.

A horse which is unable or unwilling to lie in the stable, and therefore sleeps standing, is unsound, but it may not be easy to detect such a fault in a single examination.

(*f*) Horses suffering from an enlargement of certain bursæ are unsound. A distension of the bursa of the ligamentum nuchæ, either at the poll or the withers, would be considered a definite unsoundness, even when the distension were chronic and producing no obvious ill-effect. A distended bursa of the biceps tendon would be equally unsound, although this would probably be accompanied by obvious lameness. A number of horses which exhibit "windgalls", or even distension of the synovial capsule of the knee joint, without lameness, are frequently considered to be sound and remain fit and useful. On the other hand, horses affected with synovial distensions of the hock region, such as thoroughpin and bog spavin, are classed as unsound, although many horses possess these enlargements without their usefulness being impaired.

However trivial any abnormality may appear to be, it is always wise to record it in some part of the certificate.

(*g*) All forms of arthritis, ostitis, or acute periostitis. Horses possessing a ringbone or spavin are unsound whatever influence either may exert upon the future usefulness of the animal. Many horses with well-developed spavins associated with anchylosis of the flat bones of the hock remain perfectly useful. They may carry on working throughout a normal lifetime after a preliminary spell of lameness necessitating what may be a prolonged rest. Nevertheless, they are unsound. A splint, associated with lameness, is an unsoundness. In the majority of horses over five years of age some degree of splint formation has usually become established, but in all probability any resulting lameness will have by now disappeared. Although their presence should be mentioned, small splints, causing no lameness, need not be regarded as a form of unsoundness after this age. On the other hand, any considerable exostoses resulting from them such as might be injured by the opposite foot, particularly in a horse which "goes close", would rank as an unsoundness.

Horses affected with any diseased condition of the navicular bone are unsound.

(*h*) Certain foot conditions, such as laminitis, even when chronic and not at the time of examination causing lameness, are unsoundness. These include contracted feet, although the contraction is more often secondary to some other unsoundness or defect of conformation than a primary condition. Other foot conditions, such as sandcrack, may disappear in time, but they constitute unsoundness until they do so, and similarly a false quarter, although it may never interfere with the animal's usefulness, is an unsoundness.

Sidebones are always classed as an unsoundness in spite of

the fact that in heavy horses some degree of calcification of the lateral cartilages is normally present in horses of ten years and over.

(*i*) All permanent changes in the superficial and deep flexor tendons and their synovial sheaths arising from any cause, together with those appearing in the suspensory and check ligaments, constitute unsoundness.

(*j*) A stallion is unsound if it shows any defect in its genital organs, although such defect may not interfere with the ability of the animal to sire foals.

A mare is unsound if she shows any abnormality of her genital organs, such as an enlargement of the clitoris, nymphomania or a torn perineum, but she would not be described as unsound merely because in spite of repeated services she had failed to produce a foal. She might be classed as a barren mare, but evidence pointing to this might not be available at the time of examination.

A mare which showed signs of nymphomania throughout every spring and summer might easily be passed as sound if examined in mid-winter.

The borderline between physiological and pathological demonstrations in the female is never sharply outlined.

(*k*) Certain acquired unsoundnesses may be encountered. A horse may have sustained a phlebitis or occlusion of a large vein, such as the jugular. Teeth may be missing, especially the incisors of hunters. Fetlocks or knees may have been "broken" or "chipped". Since knee injuries with fibrosis and skin adhesion indicate a tendency to fall down, they must be mentioned in the certificate, although when the degree of injury is slight they may be included among the marks of identification. Small fibrous thickenings of the skin of the fetlocks and of that overlying the metacarpal and metatarsal bones, being the result of wear and tear, may also be included as identification marks provided there is no likelihood of them interfering with the usefulness of the horse at a later date.

B

A horse which has been operated upon for roaring or whistling and has recovered raises something of a problem. In the case of a stallion if in the opinion of the veterinary surgeon the animal has been operated on for wind, a note to this effect should be added to the report. When a hunter, for instance, shows a scar or adhesion of the skin and the underlying laryngeal fascia suggestive of an operation having been performed, the fact must be mentioned in the certificate. The veterinary surgeon needs to have extremely good evidence before doing this.

Nothing in the Horse Breeding Acts will prevent the use for breeding purposes of a mare which is a roarer or has been operated upon successfully, nor is one prevented from using for breeding purposes a mare which has given birth to a cryptorchid or sexually unsound foal.

The following unsoundnesses are those laid down by the British Ministry of Agriculture and Fisheries as disqualifying a stallion for Licence under the Horse Breeding Acts, 1918 and 1948.

The horse must be free from clinical appearances of Glanders, Farcy, Dourine, Epizootic Lymphangitis, Mange, Tuberculosis, or other contagious or infectious disease.

It must be free from the following diseases and defects, viz.:

Cataract	Sidebone	Bone spavin
Roaring	Navicular disease	Stringhalt
Whistling	Defective genital organs	Shivering
Ringbone		

The veterinary surgeon is asked to say that the animal:

(a) is not lame;

(b) is lame, but not sufficiently to interfere with its usefulness as a stallion;

(c) is sufficiently lame to interfere with its usefulness as a stallion.

For the purpose of the "Report of Veterinary Surgeon" to the Ministry of Agriculture and Fisheries:

Ringbone. This term includes articular or periarticular ringbone, and any bony growth that partly or completely surrounds the pastern or pedal joints. It is not intended to be applied to well-defined, isolated exostoses on the os coronæ or lower part of the os suffraginis, commonly known as "knuckle bone" or "ankle bone".

Roaring and Whistling. If, in the opinion of the veterinary surgeon, the stallion has been operated on for wind, a note to this effect should be added to the report.

Defective Genital Organs. State defect, mentioning particularly if the horse is a "rig".

It is not the duty of the veterinary surgeon to report upon the conformation of the horse but only upon its soundness, unless it appears to him that the defect in the animal's structure is of such a nature that it will interfere with its usefulness for the purpose for which the intending purchaser requires it.

One must also bear in mind that while perfect conformation is highly desirable, many horses which fail badly in this respect frequently win races on the flat or over jumps, display speed, endurance or both these qualities, and even make good polo ponies. Not every Derby or Grand National winner is a shining example of grace and symmetry. It is desirable therefore to confine the remarks in a veterinary certificate, so far as is possible, to a simple recording of the defects which entail unsoundness. This does not imply in any way that the veterinary surgeon should be unable to distinguish between a good example of a breed and one that is inferior.

If the intending purchaser has no objection to a straight shoulder, upright pasterns and a weak loin in a heavyweight hunter it is not the business of the veterinary surgeon to raise an objection; but if the faults of conformation include a pair of calf knees and weak, sickle hocks, the question may arise as to whether these will interfere with the usefulness of the animal in such a way that they may constitute unsoundness.

Collectively, they may invalidate the performance of the animal even more than a pair of curbs, which would certainly render the animal legally unsound. It is therefore the opinion of the writer that in certain circumstances the veterinary surgeon will be justified in mentioning an extremely faulty conformation in his certificate, but it will be for him to decide whether an animal fails in conformation only in the æsthetic sense, or if the faults are likely to render the horse of little value for the purpose for which it is intended, which implies that it may be unable to stand up to its work on account of faulty conformation.

The deciding factor must be whether condemning the horse on the grounds of conformation is unjust to the vendor, or if silence is even more unjust to the client.

Considerable discussion has at times centred around this question, but no conclusion satisfactory to both parties has been arrived at, and possibly never may be.

In Britain the Ministry of Agriculture and Fisheries requires a veterinary surgeon appointed by them for the examination of stallions for licence to write a report on the conformation of the animal. At present a Ministry of Agriculture Livestock Officer also inspects the stallion and reports upon its conformation and gives his opinion upon the fitness of the animal for reproduction purposes.

In his certificate the veterinary surgeon will submit a complete list of the defects he finds and follow this with a statement detailing those defects which he considers likely to interfere with the usefulness of the animal and, so, constitute unsoundness.

He will include in this list, if detected, any one, or more than one, of the conditions mentioned in paragraphs (a) to (k) on pages 5–8.

Nevertheless, he will mention the presence of any lesser blemishes, and if he is unable to find any definite unsoundness he will be justified in saying that apart from the slight blemish or blemishes specified, the horse is, in his opinion, sound.

In addition, there are certain points to which the veterinary surgeon must give some consideration according to the circumstances of the case. One of these is the use which the potential purchaser will make of the animal and whether it is to be kept for personal requirements.

The other is with regard to the possible re-sale of the horse or pony to a third party, who may make use of the certificate given at the time of the original purchase.

The new owner may be buying the animal to ride, hunt, or exhibit, or even to drive in harness, or he may intend that his wife or child shall use it. The certificate would express the opinion of the veterinary surgeon that the animal possessed no evident unsoundness and it would be issued in the belief that any minor blemishes were not of a nature to interfere with its usefulness for the class of work for which it was required.

There is, however, a subtle difference between this qualification and that implied by the words, "the class of work for which an animal of its type might reasonably be used".

Knowing his client and his requirements, the veterinary surgeon might reasonably ascertain that the horse would do a little quiet hacking on three days of the week, that it would enjoy a little grazing in its spare time, and be stabled during a great part of the winter.

A child's pony might be intended as a first-pony, carrying the child in charge of an attendant.

But, after a week or two, the new purchaser may decide

that the horse is too frisky for his purpose, or the child may express a dislike for a slow, fat pony and demand something slim and lively. As a result both animals change hands.

Although a certificate, at least if suitably worded, constitutes part of a contract only between the veterinary surgeon and the original purchaser, the latter, who has now become the vendor, may, rightly or wrongly, make use of the certificate recently issued by the veterinary surgeon in order to assure a possible purchaser that the animal offered for sale is sound or was recently declared to be sound.

The lady's pampered hack may now become the property of a young lady who hunts it two or three days a week, rides it hard, and flogs it through or over every obstacle it encounters.

The pony may find its way into a riding school and be kept hard at work for eight hours a day at the mercy of any youngster who pays to ride it.

In this environment either animal may develop an unsoundness. The new owner may have no claim in point of law against the veterinary surgeon who issued the certificate, but may nevertheless make a determined effort to cast upon him the full blame for what has transpired. This shows clearly that the veterinary surgeon should specify in his certificate the name and address of the person on whose behalf he is making the examination, and in describing soundness or unsoundness he should include the words "at the time of my examination".

In the advertisements of sales of hunters and even of Thoroughbred stock one often sees the words, "Veterinary certificates will be lodged in the Auctioneer's Office." These animals may sometimes change hands several times in a short period, and the same certificate, taken over from the auctioneer, may accompany the horse on each occasion. Unless the veterinary surgeon covers himself in the manner suggested, a new purchaser may with some justification, perhaps, consider that he has a claim if it is discovered within a reasonable time that the horse is showing signs of unsoundness. The veterinary surgeon can base his opinion only upon what he finds at the time of his examination, and he must make this quite clear in his certificate. He is not trained to see into the future and is not qualified in the art of prophecy.

Before one can examine a horse in order to determine whether it is sound or otherwise, one must learn how to approach the animal, how to speak to it, and how to control it. Unless the veterinary surgeon is able to handle all four limbs of a horse with freedom and confidence on the occasion of first meeting it, not only will he fail to secure the confidence of the horse and his client but he will run into danger, so that his stay in veterinary practice may be short.

The student must learn the correct way to approach the horse and the safest position in which to place himself in relation to the animal while he examines various parts of its body. With practice and care he will gain experience and become familiar with the possible reactions of the horse, as well as with the reach and range of its limbs. When this knowledge has been acquired the student or young graduate will enjoy greater confidence and develop, at least outwardly, the appearance of being completely at his ease. These words are written in no flippant spirit.

The examination for soundness must never be a hurried, haphazard affair but carried out in a thorough and routine manner, in order that every point and feature of the animal may receive careful consideration.

To become successful in the examination of all kinds of livestock one must examine every part of the body in a regular sequence so that nothing is overlooked. It is quite impossible to proceed with a list of possible unsoundnesses in mind, and to dodge from one part of the body to another in haphazard fashion to determine whether any one of these unsoundnesses can be recognised. By adopting precisely the same routine in every examination one learns to see the animal in its entirety and to leave at the conclusion with no qualms concerning what one may have overlooked.

Every examiner of experience develops his own particular technique and concentrates upon its procedure, with no likelihood of being led to depart from it by interruptions from any source whatever.

It is essential also to take precautions against deception. The old-fashioned dealers have departed, and the newer type may be quite honest folk. At the same time it can do no harm to mention some of the more simple methods, calculated to mislead the veterinary surgeon, practised in the days of not so long ago.

The most common was to ascertain the time of the examination. Half an hour beforehand the horse would be taken out of the stable and exercised without causing it to sweat, then tied in the yard or box and "groomed", being made to turn from one side to the other repeatedly until the veterinary surgeon made his appearance. A horse suffering from spavin or in the early stages of navicular disease could often be brought out for inspection travelling reasonably well, its lameness temporarily reduced by the "warming-up process".

Horses affected with sandcrack, false quarter, grease or cracked heels were subjected to a different technique. The dealer "quite forgot the vet was coming", with the result that the horse would be discovered running out in an extremely muddy field or marsh, its legs caked with filth. Others would "accidentally" step or shy into a ditch while being caught or led back to the yard.

Sandcracks were frequently filled with bees' wax or candle-grease, after which the feet would be rubbed with black lead and oiled.

To disguise a small spavin, the inner surface of the opposite hock would be gently tapped a few times with a light mallet to produce a swelling which would enable the two hocks to match when their outline was viewed from either in front of or behind the horse. If the procedure caused a little lameness in the otherwise sound leg, the action of both hocks would become more alike also.

Another common trick was to hammer a stone firmly between the frog and shoe of an already lame foot. When the faulty action was noticed by the veterinary surgeon the stone would be discovered and removed. There would be an immediate improvement in the gait, and it was hoped by the vendor that the slight lameness remaining might be attributed to bruising caused by the stone.

It was wise also to watch the owner or attendant when he first led the horse out of the stable. If he held the leading rein close up under the horse's chin, kept its head high, and immediately, without being asked, trotted away up the road the suspicions of the veterinary surgeon regarding possible lameness might be justified.

If, as a result of his exertions, the handler also felt too exhausted to run again when requested to do so, or suddenly developed "lumbago", the suspicion became a little more pronounced.

These are only a very few of the methods adopted, but they may serve to put the inexperienced graduate on his guard should he discover that all the "tricks of the trade" have not disappeared.

It is always better to examine the horse at its own home rather than have it brought to the veterinary surgeon's own yard. If this is unavoidable the horse should be tied in a stall for at least half an hour before the examination commences. In its own box or stall one also sees how the horse behaves in its natural environment and may learn a great deal from the condition of its manger and of the boards beside and behind it.

One will notice whether the manger contains a lot of moisture, or "quids" of food dropped from the mouth as a result of molar troubles. The condition of the manger itself, especially if it is built of wood, will give some indication as to whether the animal is a crib-biter, a suspicion which is more feasible if the manger is covered with strips of tin or zinc. In its own box one discovers how the horse "turns over" on command, how it responds to removal of the rug (if worn) and how "touchy" it may be when an attempt is made to replace its head collar by a bridle.

If the horse is in a stall which it has occupied for some time, one can notice signs that the horse lies at night, marks caused by kicking, and, particularly, any pool of urine beneath its hind feet resulting from a hole being stamped into the floor by "itchy" legs.

Whenever it becomes possible to avoid definitely fixing a time for one's visit, it is advisable to take advantage of it. In this way one is more likely to see the horse as it really is, without preliminary exercise. It will seldom take an experienced practitioner more than from half to three-quarters of an hour to carry out a complete examination of a horse, for by following a routine method he will quickly go over the whole body and check the gait and respiration. This should not deter the less-experienced graduate from spending considerably longer and making quite sure that he has overlooked nothing.

It is wise to spend a few minutes watching the horse from the doorway of its box or entrance to its stall before it is handled by its attendant. One should never be in a hurry to have the horse brought into the open.

The practised eye learns a great deal and can see many of the animal's faults and something of its vices, if it has any. By having it turned from side to side the veterinary surgeon gains a knowledge of how the horse uses its hocks. A "shiverer", or a horse affected slightly with stringhalt, or even one in which hock flexion is restricted on account of a spavin, will frequently show symptoms in its box, particularly when turned over on a straw bed, even more readily than upon the open road after a little movement. If the box is roomy and well-lit this is often the best place in which to write down a list of identification marks and characteristics before disturbing the horse unduly. It is easier, too, to examine the mouth and dentition and determine the age at this time. Some notes on dentition as a guide to age will be found in Chapter Two.

The first glance at the horse, when one looks at it in its box, gives some indication of its type and general bodily condition. Further information regarding the latter will be obtained by placing the palm of the hand flat upon the skin covering the ribs and moving it from side to side. In a horse in good condition there is some fat beneath the skin and the underlying structures, as well as a certain amount of fluidity, so that the skin will slide freely over the ribs under pressure of the hand.

In the thin, dehydrated animal the skin appears to be glued down to the ribs and the horse is said to be "hidebound".

Although mention of poor bodily condition should be made in the certificate, one may also find evidence in some way accounting for it, such as abnormalities of the teeth, advanced age, indications of starvation, or the presence of intestinal worms, which may sometimes be observed in the horse's droppings. Thin horses should also be examined for skin parasites (such as lice or mange), although animals in good condition may also carry either of these. It is not the duty of the veterinary examiner to make a rectal examination or to take samples of fæces, but he should certainly advise the owner to call in his own veterinary surgeon, whenever he suspects that the poor condition of the horse is dependent upon the presence of parasites.

Having made out a list of the horse's identification characteristics, the veterinary surgeon will record the temperature, pulse, and respiration rate, and he will also note the respiratory movements at the flank. He will observe any evidence of undue jugular pulsation, and he will carefully auscultate the heart. This last operation will have to be repeated later after the horse has been lunged or galloped to test its wind. It is a good plan to carry a few lumps of sugar in the pocket. One of these may be given to the animal as a friendly gesture and a second lump may be "accidentally" knocked from the palm of the hand into the straw or on to the floor of the stable. This affords the examiner an opportunity to find out if the horse shows any difficulty in getting its head down to ground level. The height of the horse is usually best observed after it has been taken out of the stable, but if the floor of the box or passage happens to be level and hard, the measurement may be made indoors.

The technique of measuring is discussed on pages 19 to 23.

In 1930 the Royal College of Veterinary Surgeons published a Report of a Sub-Committee, set up by its Council in 1928, to prepare a system of colours, markings, etc., of horses for identification purposes. After twenty years experience of its use the Council decided that certain minor adjustments had become desirable.

In these circumstances they set up a Sub-Committee to reconsider the Report. This uniformity in certification of horses seemed highly desirable to the Sub-Committee for several reasons. Variations in nomenclature in different parts of the country for different breeds, and the difficulty in describing some colours are some of the factors that must receive the closest attention in providing accurate certificates of identification of horses in connection with purchase, registration, export, and insurance.

For a complete description of the "Colour and Markings of British Horses for Identification Purposes", the reader is referred to the "Report of the Sub-Committee on the Preparation of a System of Description of Colours and Markings of Horses" (December 1954), which may be obtained from the Registrar, Royal College of Veterinary Surgeons, 10 Red Lion Square, London, W.C.1. The report contains also a form of certificate and diagrams for the purpose of recording the shape, size and position of markings, which it is thought will meet the requirements of the veterinary surgeon. One will find from a perusal of this handbook that certain changes in description are made. For instance, the head markings are simplified. A horse now has a star and stripe, the old-fashioned "streak" has disappeared, but the blaze and white face remain. "Socks" and "Stockings" have gone out of use, and it is recommended that any white markings on the limbs should be accurately defined and the extent precisely stated, e.g., "white to half pastern", "white to below the fetlock", etc.

Further attention is directed to the use of hair whorls in identification. The location of whorls or irregular setting of coat hairs should be precisely indicated on the diagram accompanying the certificate. Whorls should be shown by the use of a small circle with a central dot, indicating the centre of the whorl.

It is recommended that the following order of certification should be adopted: Colour, Breed, Sex, Age, Height; marks on head (including eyes) in the order described above; marks on limbs, fore first, then hind, commencing from below; marks on body, including mane and tail; acquired marks, congenital abnormalities, whorls, or any other features of note.

The Committee is strongly of the opinion that the use of the terms "near" and "off" should be discontinued and that the terms "left" and "right" should be used exclusively.

The Measuring of Horses

The height of a horse should never be guessed if it is to be recorded in a certificate. It is a useful asset to be able to estimate the height without the aid of a staff, but it is not always completely reliable.

The nature of the ground upon which the animal stands, the thickness of the heels and soles of the veterinary surgeon's shoes and the width of the horse through the shoulders can easily account for a mistake of plus or minus one inch, quite sufficient to make all the difference between eligibility and non-eligibility to compete in a fixed-height class. Even when a purchaser has no intention of exhibiting the animal, one should not rely upon one's judgement without using a measuring staff.

In examination of a horse or pony for a private buyer the recording of the precise height may not seem a very important matter if the animal is not intended for exhibition. But purchasers may change their intentions. A young horse also tends to keep on growing, even until after it has reached six years of age.

The Joint Measurement Scheme (1956) for Children's Ponies, Hacks, Cobs, and Jumping Ponies is under the auspices of the British Horse Society, British Show Jumping Association, British Show Hack and Cob Association, British Show Pony Society, and National Pony Society.

Under this Scheme animals may be measured only between 1st April and 30th September, except when an objection may overlap this period.

Life Certificates are issued for Horses/Ponies six years old and over. The Stewards reserve the right to have an animal re-measured at any time as they may deem necessary by two Referees appointed by the Royal College of Veterinary Surgeons.

Annual Certificates are issued for Horses/Ponies under six years old. The Stewards reserve the right to have the animal re-measured at any time during the validity of the certificate as they may deem necessary by two Referees appointed by the Royal College of Veterinary Surgeons.

The following Measurement Rules have been adopted:

(1) The Veterinary Surgeon issuing the certificate has the responsibility of ensuring that the stick he uses is an accurate one; it must be fitted with a spirit level and be shod with metal.

(2) All four legs to be perpendicular to the ground, the forelegs in line.

(3) The poll shall not be lower than the highest point of the withers.

(4) The measurement shall be taken at the highest point of the withers.

(5) Measurements to be recorded as "with" or "without shoes". Ordinary shoes will permit the ½ in. allowance. No allowance to be made for tips, plates, or Charlier shoes, and such measurements to be recorded as "without shoes".

Other clauses in the scheme refer to the laying of objections and deposits and forfeits in connection therewith.

There are sometimes certain difficulties encountered when measuring ponies and horses. One is that it is essential that the floor upon which the animal stands shall be smooth, hard, and level. Smooth concrete is the best surface where it exists, and the garage floor often provides the solution. It may even be necessary at times to test the floor with a spirit level, as if the hind feet of the animal stand ½ in. lower than the fore it will often cause an equivalent lowering of the withers. The head must not be pulled down below the level of the summit of the withers, and the fore and hind limbs must be quite straight and perpendicular with no stretching out of the forefeet in a forward or of the hind feet in a backward direction.

The second difficulty may arise when one seeks the highest point of the withers. In a horse or pony with a well-laid-back shoulder and a head carried high on a muscular neck the withers may become continuous with the neck-line, and so it sometimes becomes difficult to find the highest summit of the dorsal spines. This conformation is also very common in Clydesdales and Shires. One way of getting over the difficulty is to line up the upright portion of the measuring staff with the hinder portion of the forearm. Even this method may be open to objection, as horses vary considerably in elbow placement. Some race-horses carry their elbows far forward, while many hunters carry them well back under the breast, and so the arm of the staff may vary considerably in its position on the withers.

Although the summit of the fourth dorsal vertebra theoretically represents the highest point of the withers, this is not always easy to locate. It must also be remembered that the position of the summit of this vertebra bears a direct relationship to the angle of inclination of the scapula so that in a horse with a well-laid-back shoulder it tends to lie farther back than in one possessing a straight shoulder.

Not infrequently ponies are prepared by cutting and rasping the feet to obtain the minimum height, and an extra $\frac{1}{2}$ inch is often gained by severely cutting down the hind feet.

Measuring may also present an added difficulty when the pony is suspicious that the arm of the staff may contain something sharp, such as the point of a pin. When this happens the pony will become unduly alarmed at the approach of the staff and will crouch down, and sometimes take a leap forwards as soon as the measuring arm nears the withers.

When measuring, the staff is set up so that the anterior edge of its shaft is perpendicular. The staff is then leaned towards or away from the body of the animal until the spirit level shows that the arm of the staff is perfectly horizontal, the metal foot of the staff standing firmly on the concrete

and the arm resting lightly on the summit of the withers.
The arm is then locked in position, the staff lifted off the
horse or pony and the measurement accurately recorded.

Having measured the animal and made a note of its age,
height, and identification characteristics, one may have it
brought to the doorway, where in its shade one may make a
preliminary examination of the eyes with the head facing the
light but protected from direct light from overhead. Close
one eyelid and open it again after about fifteen seconds.
Note whether the pupil has dilated and how long it takes to
contract when the eye is again exposed to light. If the horse
is arranged so that one eye faces the light and the other is
shaded, when the eye which faces the light is open the pupil
of the shaded eye contracts and when the illuminated eye is
closed the pupil of the shaded eye dilates.

Later, after the gallop, an ophthalmoscopic examination of
the eyes will be made while the pupils are dilated, but the
present superficial view of the eyes can be made with the
help of a black object, such as a bowler hat. If the veterinary
surgeon does not possess such an article an excellent substitute can be made by pasting black, non-glossy paper as
used by photographers, on to a disused table-tennis racquet.
Mydriatics to dilate the pupil are not necessary in the horse,
especially after the gallop, and in a dim light the pupil
remains sufficiently dilated for all practical purposes.

The use of atropine or homatropine may cause a dilatation
persisting for several days, and a horse treated in this way
may not be safe to ride before the pupils have again contracted.

By using the dark object so that it casts its shadow upon
the surface of the cornea, one is enabled to see any marked
opacity of the cornea which contrasts with the darkened

c

surface. Obvious cataracts can be recognised in this way, particularly if diffuse, but small localised cataracts are apt to be overlooked unless full use of the ophthalmoscope is made at a later stage of the examination.

The horse may now be led out into the yard or paddock. Notice particularly its knee and hock action as it steps out into the full daylight. A blind horse or one with defective vision (as in early cases of cataract) will usually lift the knees and feet rather higher than is usual in a horse with normal vision. It steps warily as it emerges, its ears being pricked straight forward.

The hock action may also provide some information at this time. Flexion of one or both hocks may be exaggerated when there is a tendency to stringhalt, as well as in some "shiverers".

On the other hand, one or both hocks may fail to flex in a normal fashion, and one will then be on the look-out for spavin.

A tendency to elevation of the tail and vibration of its stump is a very common feature of "shivering", and it is very frequently exhibited during the excitement caused by walking from the stable into the open.

When the horse has been brought out into the yard or paddock allow it to stand for a short while held as loosely as possible.

Watch the movement of its ears in response to sounds and observe anything suggestive of deafness.

Take note of the stance adopted by the animal when standing at ease, the position of the four feet, whether the animal stands squarely upon them or if it frequently removes the weight from one limb to its fellow. Observe any tendency to point a toe, to place it in advance of its fellow, consistently.

Any knuckling at the knees or fetlocks and any "bowing" of the back tendons must be noted, and one will observe that all the shoes are present or none, or if a shoe is audibly or visibly loose.

Look carefully at the direction in which the feet tend to point, whether they face squarely to the front, if they turn inwards (pin toes) or outwards (outbowed feet).

Notice if the hocks are close together, parallel with each other, or if they are arched outward (bow-legged).

It is now time to take a preliminary walk around the horse. Have it set in position with head up and all four feet set squarely upon the ground. Commence by standing upon its left-hand side, far enough away to be able to see the whole of this side of the animal at one time.

Note its general appearance, condition, and conformation.

Allow the eye to travel first over the outline of the animal; take notice of the head, poll, withers, back and quarters, the set-on of the tail, how this is carried, and whether it shows any tendency to quiver when the animal is spoken to or moved.

Observe the angle of the shoulder and how well or badly the scapula is placed, the ribs and girth and the angle of the haunch. Make a note of any visible abnormalities.

Next view the abdominal wall and mark the degree of "daylight" beneath the animal, whether it is a compact horse or a "leggy" creature. Observe, too, the lower line of the abdomen, whether it is low to the ground or "tucked-up" and whether there is any sign of umbilical or ventral hernia.

The limbs will next receive attention. The development of the forearm and the second thigh, the placing of the knees, fetlocks, pasterns, and feet, the length and obliquity of the pasterns, the straightness or curvature of the hocks, whether they are sickle-shaped and curby in appearance and if the tendons at the back of the cannons appear to be fine and perpendicular in outline, or whether they are thickened and "bowed". Any knuckling either at the knees or fetlocks will be particularly noted.

The skin, coat, and body surface will be considered. The

glossiness or dryness of the hair, any signs of rubbing or loss of hair from the body, mane or tail, any wounds, galls, scars, or enlargements will be recorded.

From the left side one passes to the right side of the body and makes a precisely similar examination.

Having viewed the stationary horse from either side, proceed to the front of the horse. Stand back sufficiently far that the head, neck, shoulders, and forelimbs, as well as the outline of the hips and quarters, can all be seen at one time. One then receives an impression of the general shape, whether the horse is wide or narrow in its shoulders, the amount of space between its forelimbs, whether they are set-on perpendicularly to the ground or whether they show a curvature as they descend ("Bow-legs" or "Knock Knees"). One also discovers whether the horse is streamlined, as so many Thoroughbreds are, so that one sees the outline of the hips, or whether the animal is heavy and thickset throughout. The picture will vary considerably according to the breed. Most Shires, Clydesdales, and heavy breeds generally are usually sufficiently wide in front to block the greater part of the view of the hinder half of the body. In either case, one can observe from the front of the horse any marked difference in the outline of the two shoulders and whether there is present any atrophy of the shoulder muscles, particularly of those overlying the scapula. When the atrophy appears to be unilateral, one will have to decide at a later stage of the examination whether the disparity arises from one atrophied and one normal shoulder or from one normal shoulder and one enlarged shoulder. Atrophy of the shoulder muscles may be associated with lameness of the lower part of the limb, which has resulted in a diminished use of the shoulder muscles, or it may arise from injury to the nerves supplying the suprascapular muscles. When the suprascapular nerve is involved the point of the shoulder may jut slightly outwards, and this appearance will be accentuated when the horse is trotted towards one, even when the degree of lameness is only slight (shoulder slip).

When one has any doubt regarding atrophy of the shoulder muscles on either side it is wise to step forward and grasp the belly of each mastoido-humeralis muscle at the lower end of the neck immediately above the jugular groove. Atrophy of this muscle is usually present when chronic lameness is present in any portion of the forelimb below the elbow, or when the lameness arises from a bursitis of the biceps tendon as it passes over the bicipital groove, but not so commonly when it proceeds from injury to the suprascapular nerve.

When there is wasting of the mastoido-humeralis muscle from any cause the cervical vertebræ may appear very prominent on the affected side of the neck and give the impression that the neck bones are enlarged.

Having satisfied oneself that the two shoulders are identical in shape and size when the horse stands squarely upon all its feet, one should again consider the lower limb, and particularly the knees, fetlocks, coronets, and feet. Observe carefully how the one limb is placed in relation to its fellow and whether they are perpendicularly placed and quite parallel, the one with the other.

From above downwards note any enlargement in the sternal region, the equal muscular development of the forearms, and then carefully observe the anterior aspect of the knees. These should be wide and flattened. There should be no swelling suggestive of a "bumped knee" or a hæmatoma. The skin covering them should be smooth and devoid of any scars, large or small (broken knees). One may see one or more synovial enlargements following the course of the extensor tendons as they pass over the knee below the skin, and occasionally, distensions of the synovial capsule of the knee joints bulging out between the rows of carpal bones.

All these conditions will be studied in greater detail when

each limb is examined individually, but the present superficial examination, if its findings are carefully recorded, will
help considerably in bringing to notice the more obvious
abnormalities.

While one stands in front of the horse, it is usual to stoop
and observe the outline of the forelimbs against the light
and note any enlargements on the inner or outer surface of
the knee, of the cannons below the knee, the outline of the
fetlocks, whether normally flattened at either side, or
rounded, and the shape and position of each foot.

One then looks between the forelimbs and studies the outline of the hind limbs when viewed from the front, paying
very particular attention to the outline of each hock over the
seat of spavin. Make a note of any apparent discrepancy and
pay special attention to this later when the hocks are examined individually and by comparison.

Allow the eyes to travel down the outlines of all four
cannon bones, observing any bony enlargements caused by
brushing, speedycutting, or the presence of large splints.

A great many hunters commence in life with good square,
flat-sided fetlocks which later develop thickenings of the skin
and subcutis, or even superficial bony enlargements. As
most of these are caused by contact with fence rails, stone-
walls, or wire, they are usually referred to as being the results
of "wear and tear". On the other hand, a large bony prominence, similarly produced, may be liable to injury from the
opposite foot, or may possibly expose the horse to the risk of
a fall. This interferes with the usefulness of the animal and
must be classed as an unsoundness.

The coronets and feet require especial attention. Any disparity in the outline of the two coronets should be very carefully noted. Observe whether one is larger than the other or
whether both appear unduly large, with a dissimilarity in
their respective outlines.

Compare the size and shape of the two forefeet, noticing

whether they are of normal size, too large, too small, or whether one is larger than its fellow. Notice their degree of uprightness and whether the outer and inner wall of each is of correct relative height, or if either is higher or lower on one side than is normal.

Horses occasionally own "odd feet", but although both may be sound, the condition is undesirable. One will at a later stage of the examination observe each foot in detail and determine whether one which appears smaller than its fellow is an "odd" foot or one which has contracted from other causes.

The shoes the horse wears should be noted, especially if they are unduly worn at the toes or on either side of the foot.

Next, move round behind the horse, sufficiently far to keep out of danger and enable you to see the whole of both hind limbs and the outline of the abdominal wall.

First look very carefully at the outline of the quarters and especially at each angle of the haunch. See if the two quarters match perfectly while the horse is standing level with equal weight upon each hind foot. Note whether one haunch is even slightly lower than the other ("pin down") or if the muscles of one quarter are flatter and less rounded than those of the other. Even the slightest variation may suggest the existence of lameness, past or present, in the limb corresponding with the side carrying the less-developed muscles. It is extremely important that this should not be overlooked, as hind-limb lameness may be intermittent, or may disappear when the horse is "warmed-up", and this may happen to be one of the animal's good days.

Any deformity of a pin bone (*tuber coxæ*), however little, is especially important, and its degree may be quite slight and apt to be overlooked in a fat horse when it results from a knocking-off of only one angle of the tuber coxæ. The detached portion may be loose and united to the main bone only by fibrous tissue.

Note the set-on of the tail and the straightness of its

stump, the absence of kinking or lateral deviation, and also that the horse is able to raise and lower it normally. Observe the hair upon it, especially at its root, whether it covers the tail completely and naturally, or if the hairs are broken or absent as the result of irritation and rubbing. Note the presence of any lice. In a horse at pasture a dermatitis may be present ("sweet itch"). Raise the tail and look at the anus and perineum and at the vulva in the mare. In grey horses observe the presence of any melanotic growths in the perianal region. Look now at the prominence of each buttock and see if any signs of bruising or hæmatoma exist. Observe the outline of the muscles overlying the femoral region, for if there is lameness in either hind limb these, too, may show signs of atrophy. The second thigh should be long, well-developed, and muscular, and the two thighs should correspond in this respect. Any wasting of their extensor muscles may suggest unsoundness, particularly of the hock.

The space between the inner surfaces of the thighs may vary with the bodily condition of the animal, although some horses always show a great deal of daylight between them ("cut up" thighs).

The hocks will now be inspected from behind. Approach the horse carefully, have a foreleg held up if necessary, hold the tail on one side and look downwards between the hocks. Observe the outline of their inner surfaces against the ground and carefully note any prominence over the seat of spavin and then look down the hinder edge of each from the point of the hock downwards and note whether each hock is straight and quite perpendicularly placed or if it shows a bulge indicative of a curb. Observe any undue prominence of the heads of any of the small splint bones, and also any enlargement of the point of the hock (capped hock).

The fetlocks, pasterns, feet, and the heels of both pasterns and feet will be examined in the same way as they were when dealing with the forelimbs.

The inspection of the horse from these four points, as described, may appear a lengthy and complicated procedure, but in actual practice the whole external examination occupies very few minutes, for as soon as one gains experience the eyes quite automatically take in the various features very rapidly.

It is said that the experienced veterinary surgeon will already have observed most of the defects present by the time that the horse has been led out of its box, and in many cases this is not an exaggeration, although a more detailed examination will be required to confirm any suspicions arising from a purely visual inspection.

It is unwise in surgical as in medical diagnosis to jump to hasty conclusions. Simple observation may raise one's doubts, but a final diagnosis must be based always upon careful, detailed examination and a measured consideration of one's findings.

The easiest way to attain proficiency in observation is to carry out the four-point visual examination of every horse he or she can contact and for which time permits. The routine is quickly acquired, and speed and efficiency will follow.

It is now time to have the horse moved through its various paces, but before doing this it may be well to consider the gaits of the horse and particularly its normal responses when led away from a standing position.

It is a common but a mistaken idea that lameness becomes more apparent the faster the horse moves. Often, the walk, or the fast walk, provides very useful information, while at others a slow trot will show the faults. A horse is never at its best during the fast walk; it is an unnatural pace calculated to upset the animal's balance, and must be learned by young horses. Unlike the jog trot and the fast trot, it is not a pace acquired without a deal of practice.

The standing position of the horse raises several important

considerations. Left free to its own devices, the horse seldom stands squarely upon all four feet; more usually one hind foot is held a little in front of its fellow, and one forefoot a little behind the other. There is good reason for this apparent slackness of posture.

The forelimb locks at the elbow when the joint is carrying weight because the olecranon is then contained within the olecranon fossa. At the same time the knee is held in full extension by the muscles in front of the forearm, which contract in conjunction with the flexors situated behind the forearm. As a result, when the weight of the animal rests upon the forefoot the knee and fetlock cannot be flexed or the foot lifted from the ground until the elbow has first been flexed. This, too, is impossible until the hind foot has advanced, the hock has flexed, and the weight of the body which was resting upon the forefoot has in this way been transferred to the hind foot.

When this happens the centre of gravity is shifted farther back along the body of the horse, the quarters descend as the hocks flex, and the forelimbs become free to go into action. Although this is described as though in slow motion, the whole change-over takes places very rapidly.

This explains the difficulty the young horse experiences when it is made to stand squarely on all four feet and is then asked to walk on. Being in a quite unnatural position, it is momentarily at a loss as to how best to start off, and is therefore apt to shuffle its feet until it has acquired the art. Accordingly, a deal of information can be gathered by watching any horse, experienced or inexperienced, start away from the four-square position. During the starting off, a sore limb will be distinctly favoured, and the pattern of movement will be accordingly altered. In the same way the act of pulling up to a halt is worth watching. During this procedure the horse uses the heels of the forefeet as brakes and transfers the weight of the body to the flexed hind limbs. In cases where hock or stifle flexion is impeded by arthritis the modification of the pattern of "pulling-up" can be distinctly recognised.

The horse has now started away at the walk. It will travel about twenty yards, then turn round, walk back to its starting-point, and be brought to a standstill. As it goes away observe the action, whether each limb travels forward in a straight line, how close or far apart are the hind limbs during their progress, and does the animal brush?

If both stifles and hocks are flexing freely it should be possible to see the sole and frog of each hind foot as it is raised from the ground. The same applies to the forefeet if these can be watched in their turn.

If a horse has an anchylosed hock on one side and a sound hock on the other the difference in flexion can be distinguished by the fact that the point of the hock of the affected limb is not lifted as high at each stride as that of the sound limb, and the sole and frog of the sound foot can be seen at each stride, but not in all cases can that of the lame limb be seen. When the horse turns around, watch its hock action and be on the look-out for exaggerated flexion of either hock (stringhalt), or lack of flexion (spavin?).

Notice also how clever or clumsy the animal is in turning, how it handles its feet, and whether it crosses its legs unduly.

Notice at all times where the hind feet land upon the ground—whether the pattern is correct or whether the hind foot tends to land in the print made by the forefoot (plaiting).

Notice any tendency of the horse to throw the forefeet out of line, usually by swinging them outwardly (dishing) or inwardly (brushing). As the horse returns, this may be seen more plainly, and it will also be observed whether the inner branch of the shoe appears to strike the opposite fetlock or the cannon bone immediately below the knee.

We are presuming that any lameness present will be very slight and that little of it can be seen at walking pace. In cases where the lameness is obvious the head will be seen to nod during the walk, or when the horse is walking away one quarter may drop at each alternate step.

The horse will now be trotted slowly away from the examiner for twenty yards, turned, brought back, and halted. Emphasise the fact that the animal is to turn at a certain point, otherwise you may discover that the sellers' idea of trotting is to run out of sight and to return walking and out of breath. On this occasion, as well as noting any defects in action, pay particular attention to the presence of lameness.

Forelimb lameness located below the elbow, at least, is indicated by the fact that the horse nods the head more obviously when the foot of the *sound limb* comes to the ground. When the weight of the body falls upon the lame forelimb the horse advances the sound forelimb as quickly as possible rather than maintain weight longer than possible upon the sore limb. In hind-limb lameness one watches the top line of the two quarters. In the sound horse these remain level at each stride. In the lame horse the quarter of the *sound limb* usually sinks each time the foot lands upon the ground. Viewed from the side one may also note lack of stifle and hock flexion on the lame side in cases of stifle lameness and spavin.

When a horse is lame high up in the forelimb (as in the shoulder) the head my jerk upwards when the lame limb is advanced. This type of lameness in any marked degree is unlikely to be present in a horse presented for examination.

The rule is to watch the head as the horse comes towards you and the quarters as it leaves. In the latter case watch whether one quarter drops faster and lower than the other. It is not wise, however, to depend entirely upon the rule that the quarter drops when the foot of the sound limb comes to the ground. Hip and foot lameness may sometimes produce behaviour different from that exhibited during, say, stifle or hock lameness. A good deal of information can be gained by watching the horse at rest and when slowly turned in a short circle. The detection of the lame hind limb is not always easy, and has bothered many experienced practitioners. If the hind-limb action appears normal, watch the horse turn as before, noting any abnormal flexion or lack of flexion, also its handiness or otherwise in turning.

Listen for a clicking sound during trotting, which may indicate a loose shoe if slight, but when pronounced usually means that the horse is striking the edge of the toe of the hind shoe upon the concave toe of the front shoe. Some horses "over-reach" to the extent that the concave edge of the toe of the hind shoe is carried forward so far that in descending it may sometimes strike the fleshy heel of the forefoot and cut a hanging V of skin from it during its descent. Look for evidence of this when making a detailed examination of the coronets and feet.

On occasion a horse may be lame in more than one limb; it may be lame in both forelimbs, both hind or in a fore and hind limb of the same or different sides. It is not always as easy as one might imagine to detect precisely which are the limbs involved, but in any case for the purpose of an examination it is sufficient to describe the horse as lame, and therefore as unsound at the time of examination.

If you are satisfied that the animal is not lame at the walk or the trot, have it turned several times in short circles in each direction. Watch the hock action very closely, either for stringhalt or diminished flexion. Finally, have the horse backed in a straight line for a dozen yards. A horse with spinal disorder may be incapable of backing, and one occasionally encounters an otherwise apparently sound horse which appears quite incapable of backing for no obvious reason.

The detailed examination of the horse begins at the head.

The nostrils and lips first undergo inspection. The nostrils should be widely open and any falling in of their wings noted, as must any pendulous condition of the lips arising from nerve injury. Look at the mucous membrane lining the nostrils and observe whether there is absence of inflammatory œdema, also of red spots (petechiæ). Unhealthy nasal discharge or an offensive smell from the nostrils or mouth will require investigation.

The gums, posterior to the incisor teeth of the upper jaw, may be swollen and inflamed, especially in young horses, and temporarily, at least, this may interfere with feeding.

The tongue may show abrasions on its lateral surface caused by friction or bites from sharp-edged cheek teeth. The frænum may be torn in the process of administering a ball or during attempts to rasp the teeth. Part of the tongue may be missing, and this has been recorded as occurring from the application of a twitch to the tongue by a farrier in an endeavour to control a horse during shoeing.

One must determine whether the two jaws are unequal in length, with the production of an overshot mouth (parrot mouth), or of one which is undershot, a less-common condition. Either may be overlooked unless pronounced. The age has already been recorded.

Either at the time when the age is being estimated or subsequently, it is essential to examine the cheek teeth. The tongue is drawn out and carefully held on one side of the mouth while the teeth are inspected with the aid of an electric torch, or a gag is applied and the teeth examined by the hand. Sharp edges, uneven wear, step mouth, missing teeth, caries, or teeth worn down nearly to the gums can all be detected and recorded. Defective teeth constitute an unsoundness, and may seriously affect the usefulness as well as the bodily condition of the animal. Offensive breath may be traced to caries, and sometimes is associated with a diseased alveolus and sinus infection. Missing incisors, not due to the changing of milk teeth, must be noted in the certificate.

The presence of Wolf's teeth should also be mentioned. These may be removed by the purchaser's veterinary surgeon if the new owner considers their presence harmful.

Look very carefully at the front edges of the permanent incisors and observe whether they show undue wear and a rounded-off appearance. This is suggestive of a crib-biter. Many horses "suck wind" without catching hold of any object whatever between their teeth. Instead of this, the horse usually tucks its nose in towards its chest and gulps repeatedly. Crib-biting and windsucking are vices which constitute unsoundness. A horse may be a confirmed de-stroyer of wooden mangers without being a windsucker.

The absence of the temporary corner teeth at the time the permanent laterals are making their appearance suggests that someone connected with the animal is impatient to regard it as a five-year-old. One must on no account confuse a two-year-old with a five-year-old, or a seven-year-old with a horse of eleven years. This possibility will be discussed more fully in Chapter Two.

Examine the skin overlying the false nostrils for the pres-ence of cystic formation (atheroma). The region of the frontal and maxillary sinuses should be palpated and per-cussed in case pus or neoplasm exists in their interior and any sign of bulging of the bone either in the frontal, maxillary, or nasal sites should be carefully noted.

The rami of the lower jaw should also be palpated for alveolar conditions or sinus, or for injury resulting from kicks or contact with the manger. Any enlargement of the lym-phatic glands of the intermaxillary space, or the parotid region, and any swelling overlying the guttural pouches will be observed.

The ears should both be erect and freely movable, follow-ing the direction of the eyes. In occasional instances one ear or both will lop over and be devoid of movement, and this may also accompany a similar paralysis of some of the facial muscles.

Stallions occasionally receive kicks in the face, often with damage to an eye or the nasal bones.

After examining the throat region, "cough" the horse by gently squeezing the trachea below the larynx for a few seconds. Observe the nature of the cough. It should be short and sharp in tone, repeated possibly two or three times. If it is paroxysmal, hollow, or accompanied by a long-drawn-out groaning sound, one should pay particular attention to the state of the lungs (asthma, emphysema, "broken wind").

In hunters and race-horses, in particular, examine the skin over the midline of the larynx and palpate the region carefully with the finger-tips. The skin should be movable, and any adhesions or fibrosis, or the presence of a linear scar, will give rise to suspicion that the horse may have undergone operation for whistling or roaring.

Look lower down, over the midline of the trachea, for any indications of a previous tracheotomy.

The jugular furrow is important because it contains the jugular vein, which may present a jugular pulse, a frequent sign of cardiac disorder, while the skin covering the furrow may show small scars or thickenings which may suggest that the animal has received intravenous injections either for medicinal purposes or for the induction of anæsthesia. By pressing a thumb into the jugular furrow near the base of the neck one may watch the vein fill and in this way determine whether it retains its patency or whether, as the result of injections or other injuries, it has developed a phlebitis which has impaired the flow of blood through it.

The two sides of the neck must be inspected. The cervical bones do not travel straight down the middle of the neck but curve downwards towards the jugular furrow, so that in the middle portion of the neck they lie immediately above the trachea. The prominences of their transverse processes can usually be felt with the finger tips. The two sides of the neck should match perfectly, but if one side appears more "bony" or more prominent than the other one has to decide whether this is because the cervical bones are enlarged (as may happen in tuberculosis), or whether the enlargement is apparent rather than real, and arises from atrophy of the muscles of the neck on one side. In some horses a condition of "wry-neck" may be congenital in origin, with the result that the neck bones are more prominent on the one side, and there may even be a slight concavity present on the other side of the neck. Atrophy of the muscles of one or both sides of the neck may accompany certain types of lameness. If the enlargement present is in the bones of the neck the horse will experience difficulty in lowering its head to the ground. Should the muscle be atrophied this may indicate some damage to the cervical nerves, or it may also be associated with a long-standing forelimb lameness. However, advanced cases of lameness are seldom presented for examination, so that any disparity in the two sides of the neck encountered in a horse which trots soundly is more likely to be due to injury involving the cervical nerves, damage to the bones or muscles of the neck caused by pulling back upon the halter or head-collar, or to tuberculosis of the cervical vertebræ. It is wise to palpate the trachea, as occasionally one or more cartilaginous rings may be depressed or broken, especially in jumpers and hunters, either as the result of colliding with the top rail of a fence or as the result of a previous tracheotomy. A damaged ring may cause interference with breathing at fast paces.

The skin of the neck may show small fibrous thickenings due to thorn punctures or fly-bites, or to recent hypodermic injections. An urticarial rash may be present, especially in stabled horses. The presence of any form of skin irritation must be noticed.

Lice, when present, are more easily detected below the mane, on the withers, and at the root of the tail.

Place the hand beneath the horse's chin and gently raise the head as far as possible and hold it in that position for thirty seconds. When you release it, have the animal moved

D

forward a few paces. Note if there is any tendency to stagger. If there should be, examine the heart very carefully and repeat the head-lifting after the gallop.

Now pass the hand to the region of the poll, working always from the left side of the horse. Many horses resent interference with this region. Decide whether any resistance is purely temperamental, or if soreness or enlargement of the bursa overlying the axis exists. Bruising is not uncommon, and may lead to poll-evil. Bursitis is also usually accompanied by a disinclination to lower the head to graze.

Carry the hand down the crest of the neck until it rests upon the withers. Note any hyperæsthesia exhibited if the neck is handled immediately in front of the withers and palpate the summits of the dorsal spines in this region for evidence of bruising. A rather soft, fluid enlargement of one or both sides of the neck in front of the withers may indicate the existence of a bursitis of the ligamentum nuchæ which may terminate in fistulous withers.

On the back behind the withers, feel the summits of the dorsal bones for saddle bruising and palpate the area of skin underlying the saddle in riding horses for galls or for "sitfast".

Continue along the back to the angle of the haunch, palpate this, and then apply gentle pressure to the external trochanter of the femur.

The examiner should now move to the right side of the horse and carry out an exactly similar inspection of that side of the body .

Having examined the head, neck, and trunk, the veterinary surgeon will pass on to the more detailed examination of each limb. In doing this he will commence by standing on the left side of the horse facing its head, and examine the left forelimb. He will then examine the right forelimb and compare the two forelimbs before proceeding to examine the two hind limbs in similar order. It is better to carry out the examination in this way than to proceed, as many do, from forelimb to hind limb of the same side, as comparison is so much more easily made by the former method.

From the left of the horse examine the shoulder of that side. Note the position of the scapular spine and the development of the muscles lying on either side of it. It is as well next to examine the right shoulder and compare the two. Muscular atrophy, characterised by shrinking of the muscle tissue within the supra- and infra-scapular fossæ, may arise from damage to the suprascapular or infrascapular nerves, or to lameness of the corresponding forelimb of a chronic nature. The mastoido-humeralis may be palpated above the jugular furrow. Even a very slight, *chronic* lameness of a forelimb will in time induce atrophy of this muscle.

The point of the shoulder may appear a little more prominent on the one side than on the other. Any wasting of the shoulder muscles will give a fictitious prominence to the shoulder joint and to the overlying bicipital tendon. The shoulder of the sound limb will be generally fuller and rounder, as its muscles will be better developed, and so one then has to decide whether the smaller of the two shoulders is the subject of a generalised muscle atrophy from lameness low down in the limb, or if it is only the muscles overlying the scapula which are involved as the outcome of a local nerve injury. In the latter case there may be only slight lameness with some abduction of the shoulder; in the former case the lameness will usually be more evident.

At the point of the shoulder the biceps tendon passes through the bicipital groove in the head of the humerus, and as this is the most prominent part of the body as it advances, it is subjected to risk of traumatic injury. A bursitis at this spot causes lameness, and a horse with an acute bursitis would not be presented for examination for soundness. It is possible, however, to encounter horses showing quite mild symptoms, of which the owner would like to dispose.

Few sound horses relish any heavy digital pressure over the bicipital groove, and one must not imagine that every horse which flinches when this is applied is necessarily unsound. One can gain some help by palpating both shoulders and comparing results.

The elbow joint is seldom the seat of unsoundness, but the point of the elbow is not infrequently bruised by contact with the inner heel of the shoe while lying. It may then develop a hæmatoma which may later become fibrosed, with the formation of a hard, rounded swelling which often contains or discharges pus (capped elbow).

Excoriation of the axillary region may be encountered, especially in fat draught horses, or a girth gall may be met with immediately behind the elbow, or just above the sternal cartilage. In a horse of good conformation the girth takes up a position 2 in. behind the point of the elbows and does not drop into the space beneath them. If desired, one may extend and flex each elbow joint. This can be done only if the foot is raised from the ground and the knee flexed. The inner heel of each foot will touch the point of the elbow if there is nothing present to hinder full knee and elbow flexion.

The forearm should be long, strong, and muscular, and although it is largely concerned with pulling the body forward during all paces, it seldom shows unsoundness.

Each knee should be flat and broad, with a well-developed pisiform bone to provide a wide carpal sheath for the passage of the flexor tendons. Any synovial distension at this point should be recognised and recorded in the certificate.

Distension of the carpal sheath may be evinced by the presence of two soft swellings above the knee, one on its inner and one on its outer surface. A third swelling may appear below the knee surrounding the upper half of the flexor tendons, extending part way down the cannon.

Distension of the sheath of the external flexor of the metacarpus appears as a swelling on the outer aspect of the knee and the lower third of the forearm immediately above the pisiform bone. It may attain the size of a hen's egg.

The sheaths of the various extensor tendons as they pass over the knee may become distended. Elongated swellings then appear along their course. Occasionally one meets with distensions of the synovial capsule of the knee joint protruding between the carpal bones. The importance of all these synovial distensions in the vicinity of the knee will depend upon size and position and the degree in which they interfere with flexion and extension of the knee joint. Frequently they cause no appreciable lameness, but in every case their existence should be recorded in the certificate. Broken knees usually indicate that the horse has fallen, but unless one knows the circumstances connected with the incident it is difficult to say whether it is likely that the fall will be repeated. The presence of fibrosis with close attachment of the skin of the knee to the underlying joint tissues may possibly make falls more likely.

Broken knees are far less commonly encountered now than they were years ago when horses were driven in harness on badly made roads.

Hæmatoma (bumped knee) or hygroma, in which there is a considerable fibrosis present, may result from lying on a bad floor or from a habit of striking the manger with the knee when pawing in the stable at approach of meal-times. These seriously interfere with knee flexion.

Carpal exostoses, knee splints, may be an extension from ordinary metacarpal splints to the head of the small metacarpal bone.

The metacarpal region provides two areas for close inspection. The first is the line of demarcation or of union, between the large and small metacarpal bones. Inflammatory changes at their junction gives rise to pain and lameness, more commonly in young horses. Calcification of the interosseous ligament follows, and fusion takes place at various points. As soon as the degree of anchylosis is sufficient to prevent further movement between the bones the lameness generally disappears, but a palpable bone deposit (splint) will remain. If this is sufficiently large on the medial surface of a limb to be hit by the opposite foot, lameness may result. Large exostoses in the region of the knee or cannon must therefore be classed as unsoundness. The splint may extend to the knee and cause interference with its movement, or it may pass beneath the suspensory ligament and cause friction or tearing, with lameness.

Sore shins result from localised periostitis of the large metacarpal bones and occur in young horses exercising or working on hard ground. Pain is evinced when the surface of the metacarpal bone is pressed by the fingers, and sometimes a thickening of the periosteum can be palpated.

Concussed knees are common in jumpers, but are difficult to diagnose. They cause the horse to take its jumps obliquely at first and later to refuse.

The structures at the rear of the cannon bone, which require close attention are: (1) the suspensory ligament; (2) the check or subcarpal ligament; (3) the deep flexor tendon (perforans); (4) the superficial flexor tendon (perforatus).

The perforatus is the largest and thickest of the group. It is not always possible to differentiate the various layers by palpation except in thin-skinned horses. One should be able to insert the tips of the fingers between the deep flexor tendon and the front edge of the cannon bone when the knee is flexed, but this cannot be done when an inflammation of the tendons has resulted in the formation of adhesions between the skin and underlying structures. The finger-tips, thus inserted, will rest on the edge of the check ligament immediately below the back of the knee in a sound horse, while in the lower half of the cannon they make contact with the suspensory ligament.

It is not easy to find the line of demarcation between the

superficial and deep flexor tendons excepting for a distance of 1–2 in. at the centre of the cannon, beneath the carpal sheath, and above the sesamoid sheath. At this spot the perforatus is devoid of a synovial covering. The veterinary surgeon will palpate the tendons of each foreleg in turn and decide whether they are identical in each and normal to the touch. They may have become thickened and more fibrous as the result of a preceding attack of tendonitis or tendosynovitis. When the superficial flexor (perforatus) is contracted and thickened, the normal straight edge at the rear of the tendons is lost and is replaced by a raised, curved surface (bowed tendons), and there will be knuckling of the fetlock although the foot will rest flat upon the ground.

When the heel is raised from the ground and the fetlock is knuckled it indicates that contraction has occurred in the deep tendon (perforans). It is quite possible that some contraction of the superficial tendon may be present without the manifestation of very obvious lameness.

Thickening of the check ligament, resulting from strain, can usually be palpated as a hard swelling close to the metacarpal bone extending from the back of the knee to about 4 in. below it. Usually this causes lameness, but the horse presented for examination may have recovered from the painful condition, while the thickening and fibrosis persists. This is a very definite unsoundness. As it is rather unusual for two check ligaments to be affected simultaneously, a comparison of the two limbs will be helpful. When the suspensory ligament is subjected to intense strain it may rupture partially or completely. In this event the sesamoids will drop, and the fetlock will sink down closer to the ground than that of the sound limb. The foot will nevertheless remain flat upon the ground. At first the lameness will be severe, but later in many cases it will diminish or almost disappear, leaving, however, the "dropped fetlock". The "broken-down" race-horse is a common example of an animal in which the suspensory ligament has undergone a severe stretching process, sometimes amounting to rupture. Rupture of the perforans tendon will result in the horse travelling on its heel with the toe in the air, while rupture of the perforatus produces marked knuckling of the fetlock with the foot remaining flat upon the ground. It is unlikely that any such cases of this sort will be brought in for examination for soundness, although many strained tendons and check ligaments recover to such an extent that the horse may change hands, often more than once, so one must be on the look-out for horses carrying these common types of unsoundness.

On the inner head of the first phalanx (suffraginis), one may meet with an exostosis (cab-horse disease) which constitutes a definite unsoundness. The lameness diminishes or departs with rest, but the enlargement remains, and may easily be missed in a horse "warmed-up" for the occasion. The fetlock may be enlarged and rounded from wear and tear, or it may carry "brushing marks" or actual wounds on its medial aspect. High up on the inner aspect of the cannon bone one may discover a bony enlargement, often with accompanying skin injury associated with "speedycutting". Any of these injuries resulting from striking the limb with the opposite foot, or its shoe, must be recorded.

Other skin injuries in the metacarpal area may be caused by rapping the limb on jumps, or by damage by thorns or wire. If the skin injuries are purely superficial and cause no lameness they may be entered in the certificate as the result of wear and tear, or they may often be included as identification marks.

The sesamoid bones may become inflamed, undergo rarefaction, and may eventually fracture. In the early stages of a simple sesamoiditis the horse will be lame, but after a month at grass it may come in sufficiently fit to be offered for sale. Careful comparison of the two fetlocks in the sesamoid area should provide some evidence of unsoundness. It remains a fact, however, that the most difficult lesions to detect are those which exist below the knees, and it is a curious fact that when a horse is slightly lame on the two limbs of one side the lameness is often more difficult to detect than when only one limb is unsound.

Experienced veterinary surgeons have always maintained that the fetlocks, coronets, and feet are the commonest seats of unsoundness and also provide the greatest risk of error. The presence of articular abnormalities and the detection of small exostoses in the first and second phalanges is not always easy until the condition has progressed until enlargements become visible, or at least easily palpable. The foot of the horse offers even greater difficulty.

Until recent years we were without the advantages of X-ray diagnosis, and although few veterinary surgeons travel to examine horses for soundness equipped with a portable set by which they may take films and develop them on the spot, they can certainly resort to this means of diagnosis when doubt arises.

In the majority of cases, however, the certificate will be based upon what the veterinary surgeon discovers by the aid of his eyes, ears, and fingers, and the diagnosis he makes will depend largely upon his personal knowledge and experience.

The pasterns and coronets are palpated with the fingertips, using the thumb to maintain the exact degree of pressure required. In most cases this will be very slight, in fact the more experienced the examiner, the lighter will be the touch.

In examining the coronets one stands at the side of the horse facing its head, using the right hand to palpate the left coronet and the left hand to palpate the right coronet. One may view both coronets occasionally from the front for comparison, but all palpation is done from the side and never from in front of the horse's forefeet, or behind its hind feet.

In palpating to detect the absence or presence of exostoses in the region of the coronets one must learn to distinguish those which surround the articular edges of the bones forming the joint, and are probably associated with true articular lesions, from exostoses which are merely outgrowths from (or deposits upon) the surface of the shaft or body of the bone, and less likely to be associated with ulceration of the articular cartilages. In order to attempt to discriminate, one must first be intimately acquainted with the anatomical outlines of the particular joint and able to trace the line of demarcation between the bones with the finger-tips. It is wise to change sides frequently, or even to compare the two coronets by palpating each in turn from one side of the horse. Occasionally, a fairly smooth and regular enlargement of one coronet can be recognised more easily by looking at the two coronets from a few yards in front of the horse than by actual palpation, especially by those whose tactile perception is still in process of training.

Both articular and non-articular exostoses may cause lameness, although animals with the latter type of enlargement often go quite sound after a rest in spite of the fact that the exostosis remains. The lameness, however, is apt to recur when the horse enters a new home and indulges in a fresh type of work.

"Anklets" are outgrowths of bone from the sides and lower ends of the first phalanx (suffraginis). They may be quite large and prominent and yet produce no permanent lameness. Other coronet exostoses may arise from treads in double harness, or from strain in horses which plough with one foot in the furrow.

The presence of a bony exostosis, whatever its position and nature, must be mentioned in the certificate. How much one will differentiate the various conditions will depend upon the veterinary surgeon's skill and experience. The young graduate will be wiser merely to state the existence of a bony enlargement on the right or left coronet and leave it at that. The most one can possibly say is that the enlargement surrounds the joint, or that in the opinion of the examiner the enlargement is an "anklet", or that it does not appear to involve the joint. One can usually determine whether the exostosis is high up in the coronet or whether it is low down, causing some bulging of the coronary band, in which case it is likely to be a "low ringbone" extending to the pyramidal process of the third phalanx (the pedal bone).

Ringbone is a somewhat vague term which when correctly used refers to true articular ringbone with joint involvement. The Ministry of Agriculture refuse to license a stallion which possesses an articular or periarticular ringbone that partly or completely surrounds the pastern or pedal joints, but they do not apply the term "ringbone" to well-defined, isolated exostoses on the lower part of the os suffraginis commonly known as "knuckle bone" or "ankle bone".

X-ray diagnosis is not always very easy to interpret in early cases of ringbone. At this stage the swelling is in existence sometimes for several weeks as an inflammatory condition of the bone, its periosteum, and the overlying tissues. An X-ray film taken at this time may show nothing. Later, when mineral salts have become deposited, the exostosis is clearly discernible—and also palpable.

It is unusual, nowadays, to perform neurectomy for the relief of lameness occurring in the coronet, but years ago it was a common operation, and many horses which had been "un-nerved" were sold by dealers. It was, and still may be, necessary to guard against passing as sound, without recognition of the fact, a horse which has been subjected to this operation. Testing the sense of feeling by pricking the coronet is not altogether reliable in horses in which the operation was carried out a year earlier. In any case, a little sensation may remain at the midline in front of the coronet, so that any pricking should be done at the inner and outer sides of the coronet. In addition, a depression or scar may be felt at the site of operation in most cases.

The length and degree of inclination of the pasterns is more a matter of conformation than of soundness, but it has also a direct bearing upon the probable duration of the horse's usefulness. Upright pasterns, especially when coupled with an upright shoulder, do little to minimise concussion, and a heavyweight hunter or a draught horse with big feet, a heavy tread, and short upright pasterns, can almost certainly be depended upon to eventually develop lameness from exostoses of the coronet region, or other lameness associated with the effects of undue concussion. On the other hand, a riding horse possessing long, oblique pasterns, little or no heel, and a considerable degree of activity, will frequently develop navicular disease if kept in regular work.

The feet must be examined from two angles, first from a few yards in front of the horse, and then from the side of the horse at close range.

If the two feet do not match exactly in size, shape, character, and in the angles of inclination of their walls, one may have to decide between "odd feet" and a contracted foot in company with one normal foot.

Atrophy of a foot is often a sequel to lameness and results from loss of sole and frog pressure.

In "odd feet" there may be a congenital disparity in their size or shape, or there may be a tilting of one foot either in an inward or outward direction. In feet of this kind there will also be unequal wear of the two sides of the foot. In odd feet, which are otherwise sound, the soles, bars, and frog will be quite normal, but in a contracted foot, in which the pumping action of the frog has been lost, there will be very little space left between the frog and the bars; the foot will be narrow, especially at its heels, and the heel of the foot, or whatever horny heel exists, will usually be turned under the wall.

In Shires the feet are large and frequently flat. The heels

are often low and poorly developed. Clydesdales usually possess even larger and flatter feet than Shires, but often the horn is of better quality and there is frequently more indication of a heel. The Percherons and Suffolks have smaller feet, usually with good heels and concave soles, and an excellent type of horn.

Shires, more so than Clydesdales, hammer their feet up and down upon the hard roads, and a great deal of concussion is transmitted through their coronets. They develop "anklets" with a fair degree of regularity. Clydesdales are a little less subject to coronary trouble, as they take a longer stride, while Percherons and Suffolks are far less liable to coronary unsoundness in the experience of the writer.

In heavy horses calcification of the lateral cartilages proceeds from nine to ten years onwards as a natural event, but to a less extent in light horses unless they are crossbreds, as are most heavyweight hunters which frequently develop some degree of calcification of their lateral cartilages after ten years of age.

A horse in which the lateral cartilages are calcified to a degree which can be easily palpated is said to possess sidebones, which are generally considered to cause unsoundness, although it is doubtful if a sidebone causes lameness unless it is abnormally developed, confined to one side of the foot, or associated, as frequently it may be, with a ringbone, or some type of coronary exostosis.

Two methods may be made use of to determine the degree of calcification present in the lateral cartilage. By the first, the heels of the coronets are palpated above the coronary band with the foot firmly resting on the ground. Each cartilage is gently pressed downwards and inwards to determine the degree of elasticity remaining in its substance and to decide whether the cartilage has become replaced by bone.

Calcification commences at the anterior end of each

cartilage where it is attached to the wing of the pedal bone, and travels backwards throughout its length until the whole structure is involved.

By the second method the foot is raised from the ground and the upper edge of the cartilage is grasped between fingers and thumb and moved from side to side.

In rare instances the bony enlargement becomes very large, frequently affecting one cartilage only. Sidebone is to be included in the certificate as an unsoundness.

Sandcrack, originating at the coronary band and extending through a part or the whole of the length of the wall of the foot, must be looked for with care. It appears more usually at the quarters of the forefoot and down the anterior midline of the wall of the hind foot. Lesser cracks, not reaching to the coronary band, may often be discovered travelling from the ground surface of the wall for a varying distance in an upward direction. It is always wise, when possible, to have all four feet washed down with a hosepipe, or scrubbed with a brush. Faking sandcracks is not an uncommon practice.

Notice carefully the shape of the feet and the depth of horn at the heels. Although the shape of the heels appertains to conformation, one is quite justified in mentioning in the certificate that the horse possesses weak heels. They predispose to corns and to navicular disease, especially in hunters and hacks. In draught horses, shoeing and the occasional use of calkins may make the defect less obvious. A hunter should possess at least an inch of sound horn at each heel above the ground surface of the foot, and between it and the skin of the coronet. More would be even better, for when the heel is low the horn available tends to enfold itself beneath the foot.

Ponies with upright walls and deep heels seldom go lame in the feet unless they are overfed and housed, when they become subject to laminitis.

In days gone by it was a routine practice to employ a farrier to remove and replace the shoes of the forefeet at the time of examination, and to pare out the heels in a search for corns. Farriers, as well as horses, were then more plentiful.

Nowadays, although many veterinary surgeons may be quite capable of removing a shoe, replacing it in a skilled manner is less easy. As in many instances the nearest farrier may be ten to fifteen miles distant, one has to do without his services in most cases.

The way to discover a corn is to pare away the horn in successive, thin layers from the angle between the bars and the wall. If a corn is present the deeper layers will show a stain, reddish in a recent case, due to bruising and hæmorrhage between the sensitive and horny layers. In older cases the colour may range from yellowish to violet. In a "moist corn" the underlying tissues are infiltrated with serum, and in a suppurating corn pus will be present, together with pain and lameness.

A so-called "dry corn" is one in which bruising has been occurring in a mild way for some time. If the horse has been newly shod the lameness may be less marked, but will increase when the heel of the shoe wears thinner. Wide, open heels carrying a good depth and thickness of horn seldom develop corns, as contracted feet with weak or unturned heels so often do. In these days, too, there is difficulty in having shoes removed and the feet trimmed at proper intervals. As the foot grows and lengthens at the toe, the heels of the shoe creep forward until they rest upon the seat of corn.

It is always wise when examining the foot to run the searching knife along the lateral and central lacunæ of the frog to ensure that no nails, screws, or stones are embedded within them. At the same time any tendency to thrush or canker will be recorded.

Each foot should be tested in turn with the hammer, not

only to detect soreness, but also because the hammer may reveal a shiverer.

The manipulation of the hammer requires practice. It should never be applied too heavily. Every horse will hold its foot off the ground if it is hammered with a loud "rat-a-tat-tat", which alarms the animal. The hammer should be applied at first very gently and with intervals of a couple of seconds between each blow. The tapping should be carried around each foot. In very nervous horses it may be advisable to hold up the opposite forefoot while the foot upon the ground is being gently tapped. When the horse has become used to the hammering, lift each of the four feet (both fore and hind) in turn, and tap the soles moderately hard once or twice. A confirmed shiverer will often draw up the foot as far as possible with exaggerated flexion of the hock and stifle, often to such an extent that the horse is in danger of losing its balance. At the same time the tail will quiver.

Navicular disease in its early stages is difficult to diagnose, and many affected horses come out of the stable slightly lame but may be trotting away normally after moving a short distance. Navicular disease has proved to be much more common than was believed years ago. At rest, the animal may tend to point a toe or point both forefeet alternately. When lame, the horse travels "on its toes", taking short strides with an inclination to stumble. On account of the "pottery" action and the shortened stride, the layman's diagnosis is almost invariably shoulder lameness.

Most horses nowadays have their feet "dubbed", their toes being kept short, but in spite of this the horse with navicular lameness almost invariably wears the toes of the shoe first, since it tends to drag the toe rather than to lift the foot and stride out.

The veterinary surgeon will be well advised never to be too dogmatic in declaring the case to be one of navicular disease unless he can confirm his suspicions by X-ray ex-

amination of the feet. The diagnosis may even then be difficult, but the presence of appearances of bone rarefaction or
osteophyses should confirm it. The recognition of navicular
disease has become much more frequent since the technique
of X-ray diagnosis has improved.

When examining the sole of the foot after the shoe has
been removed, one may sometimes discover the presence of
a horn tumour (keratoma) or of "seedy toe". Horn tumour
commences at the coronary band, and from there a growth of
horn may gradually extend down to ground level, underlying
the natural horn and causing lameness. It usually produces
a visible bulge of the wall in the midline of the foot.

Seedy toe is characterised by the development of a cavity
in a similar position to that occupied by a developed keratoma, containing a powdery or pumice-like secretion which
replaces the natural firm horn. The cavity can be exposed by
paring the sole at the toe, and frequently a hollow note is
heard when the wall at the toe is lightly struck with a
hammer. Seedy toe is an unsoundness, easily overlooked.
A bulge which travels down the centre of the anterior surface of the foot starting from the coronary band or coronet,
may result from the presence of a low ringbone.

Flat soles may result merely from bad conformation, although flatness or "dropping" of the soles may be associated
with laminitis. Before declaring soles to be flat one should
carefully attempt to pare away or "dig out" the outermost
layer. If this comes away easily in loose flakes, one may find
that the apparent flatness of the sole is due to the retention of
the cast-off worn-out layers and that a little scraping and
paring will show the degree of concavity to be normal. When
a convex or truly flattened sole exists it will be impossible to
restore its natural concavity in this way.

Rings surrounding the wall of the hoof in concentric
manner may be due to seasonal variations in diet; for example, one encounters "grass rings" which arise from an

E

increase in horn secretion while the animal is at pasture. An increase or decrease in the iodine content of the fodder will be recorded on the surface of the wall of the foot in the same way Laminitic rings are more pronounced and usually accompany a flat or convex sole, together with some deformity of the foot. Frequently, the wall of the foot develops a "waist", and the toe may exhibit a tendency to grow in an upward direction. Such cases are seldom presented for examination.

Having examined the forelimbs, one will proceed to an inspection of the abdominal wall, particularly for any type of hernia, such as ventral or umbilical hernia.

The groin in the male animal, and even in the gelding and mare, requires very close examination.

In the adult entire horse, as well as in foals and colts up to three years of age, one must make a careful search for scrotal hernia. Inguinal hernia may also exist, and upon the degree of its protrusion through the external ring will depend the ease or difficulty associated with its detection.

In the foal a wide inguinal canal may permit the passage of omentum and possibly small intestine into the tunica vaginalis, and this may distend the scrotum, which may hang down almost to the level of the hocks. This is often assisted by the presence within the tunica of a considerable quantity of fluid (hydrocele). By the time the foal has reached twelve months old, all this protrusion of the tunica vaginalis and its contents will not infrequently have disappeared. An inguinal hernia may, nevertheless, remain. When this is not apparent at the inguinal ring a rectal examination, when feasible, may give some information, but for purpose of the present examination this will not be required, unless expressly asked for by the purchaser, and carried out with the consent of the owner.

In the adult stallion scrotal hernia may vary in size from time to time according to the nature and volume of its contents and the strength and irritability of the cremaster muscle. It is usually more visible after exercise.

The schirrous cord may first become evident months or even many years after castration, and at first may take the form of a hard mass which can be detected by deep palpation of the inguinal region. Later it becomes larger, causes lameness, and may develop into an abscess which bursts, leaving a sinus.

In occasional instances one may detect in the gelding a soft, fluctuating swelling, apparently underlying the "dimple" or scar left by castration. This is a cystic condition of the divided end of the spermatic cord.

In the entire, from a year onwards, the formation and descent of the testicles must be carefully checked. In order to determine whether a colt or adult stallion is sound or unsound in its genital organs, one has to determine whether a normal pair of testicles rests upon the floor of the scrotum—not always so easy to decide in a lively stallion. The horse possesses a fairly wide inguinal canal and powerful cremasters, and in moments of excitement, whether sexual or induced by the presence of a stranger, one or both testicles of a perfectly normal animal may be drawn up into the inguinal canal. This will frequently happen whenever an attempt is made to palpate the testicle with the hand, particularly in cold weather. For this reason one must be careful not to condemn a stallion as being a cryptorchid, unilateral or bilateral, until after it has been lunged for its wind. If the horse is really warm and tired from its exertions the testicles should make their appearance, if they are capable of descending into the scrotum.

It is sometimes better to repeat the examination of the genital organs after the lapse of a week, as some stallions, not at all unsound, display seasonal or temperamental characteristics so far as the position of their testicles within the inguinal canal and the scrotum is concerned. If the testicles are palpable, care must be taken to see if they are well developed, of approximately the same size (the left one may be normally slightly the larger), and whether each spermatic cord is of sufficient length to permit the testicle to descend completely onto the scrotal floor. If one testicle lies freely within the scrotum and the other, even after the gallop, remains suspended at the entrance to the external inguinal ring, the stallion will be said to possess one incompletely descended testicle. (Say whether right or left in the certificate.) At the time this will be an unsoundness, but if the animal is a two- or three-year-old it should be re-examined after the lapse of a few months before declaring it to be permanently unsound.

When only one testicle is visible an examination can be made, if the animal is sufficiently quiet, to determine the presence or absence of an operation scar or "dimple".

It is sufficient, however, to record in the certificate that only one testicle (right or left to be stated) could be found at the time of examination.

In the mare the mammary gland must be palpated to determine whether it is normal in size, shape, and texture, whether the teats are normal and free from induration, and if the glands are free from mastitis.

Proceeding to the hind limbs, one will see that both quarters are of equal size and shape. This, together with an examination of the haunch bones, has already been carried out. In cases where any atrophy of the gluteal muscles is present, marked attention must be paid to the lower part of the limb, especially to the hock joint.

If the subject is a mare, note any tendency to "flash" the clitoris and at the same time liberate small quantities of urine, any tendency to squeal or exhibit other sexual proclivities. Such behaviour may merely mean that the mare is in œstrus, particularly in springtime, but, certainly, in mid-winter it would lead one to suspect the existence of ovarian disorder and nymphomania.

Examine each hind limb completely and then compare any parts, such as the stifles or hocks, which raise any suspicion of being in any way abnormal. The external trochanter of the femur is easily located, but the hip joint lies deeper and is out of reach. Bruising of the trochanter occasionally occurs, and lameness may persist in greater or less degree for a very long time.

The stifle should now be examined for synovial distension. This may exist over the patella when the superficial bursa has met with an injury, frequently as the result of a kick.

Synovial distension of the femoro-tibial and patellar joints is usually manifested on the outer aspect immediately behind the patella, below the patella in front of the limb, and less commonly on its internal aspect. The degree of lameness is very variable, and quite frequently there is very little, if any, very noticeable lameness present. In more acute cases the lameness may be severe.

A greater difficulty may arise in detecting intermittent subluxation of the patella, which is often shown only during trotting, cantering, or galloping. In two- and three-year-olds, especially when the stifles and hocks are exceedingly straight, the patella may slip partly off the trochlea of the femur and become held up upon the lateral ridge, and less usually upon the upper part of the condyle. This causes a momentary immobility of the limb. In the former case it remains for a few seconds in a state of flexion, and when the patella rests upon the upper part of the trochlea the limb goes into extension. As a rule, the animal checks, hops a few steps on three legs, the patella slips back into its trochlear groove, and the gait is restored to normal. This may happen several times while the animal is travelling half a mile, or it may occur more or less frequently according to the individual case. On this account a mild degree of stifle subluxation is a condition which might unfortunately be overlooked. When a raw colt is being lunged in a circle on a rope the gait is often somewhat ungainly, and an inexperienced observer might easily attribute a momentary subluxation to awkwardness on the part of the animal.

In older horses subluxation is not nearly so common, and it would appear that the condition is associated with bone length/growth, and that it frequently disappears when the final relative length of bones is attained with adult age. In any case it is rarely seen excepting in animals bred (as so many are today) possessing exceptionally straight stifles and hocks, with a view to greater speed.

The stifles should just clear the skin of the flanks at fast paces without any tendency to turn in an outward direction. When there is undue friction excoriation of the skin inside the limb may occur in hot weather. When the stifles turn excessively outwards the horse is said to "punch the stifles".

The direction of travel of the stifle joint is influenced by the degree of obliquity of the grooves of the astragalus. When the points of the hocks are set wide apart the stifles will turn inwards and friction may result. When the points of the hocks are turned inwards (cow hocks) the stifles will be punched outwards.

The fingers should travel down the length of the inner surface of the tibia to ensure an absence of tibial bruising at its exposed parts. When approaching the hock feel carefully beneath the perforans tendon on both its inner and outer sides at the entrance to the tarsal sheath to see if a bursal enlargement protrudes (thoroughpin).

"Articular thoroughpin" is a term sometimes used to describe a bulging of the capsule of the true hock joint occurring at the hollow of the joint, between the lower end of the tibia and the os calcis. This may extend through the joint and appear also upon its outer aspect so that digital pressure upon one side of the swelling causes increased distension of the other side. Thoroughpins vary in size from week to week. They become smaller in winter and after prolonged rest. It is seldom that they produce lameness. The presence of a thoroughpin constitutes unsoundness.

Chronic bog spavin is a common condition, also arising from distension of the synovial capsule of the true hock joint and it is often associated with articular thoroughpin. It produces a soft distension at the antero-internal aspect of the joint which may attain a considerable size. The importance of these synovial distensions depends upon the degree to which they interfere with hock flexion. Unless very large, they seldom cause lameness, and although they may do little to lessen the animal's usefulness, they are, nevertheless, classed as unsoundnesses and must be described as such in the certificate.

Two other synovial distensions may be encountered in the hock region. One affects the sheath of the peroneus tendon on the outer side of the cannon bone; the other the sheath of the accessory flexor on the inner side of the hock. Neither causes lameness, but they must be recorded in the certificate.

Capped hock may be a serious blemish and an unsoundness when well developed. A very slight, chronic enlargement of the point of the hock may be included in the identification.

The least-harmful type arises from an inflammation of the mucous or subcutaneous bursa lying between the skin and the perforatus tendon at the point of the hock. The more serious type occurs when a distension exists in the synovial bursa underlying the cap of the perforatus, between it and the tuber calcis. This causes lameness.

The identification of a small spavin was ever the bugbear of the young graduate, and still gives rise to differences of opinion among the more experienced.

"Odd hocks", not in any way unsound, are quite common in horses, and the difficulty lies in deciding whether an apparent difference in the hocks is normal or an unsoundness, and if due to unsoundness, which of the two hocks is unsound.

The first essential is that the student or graduate shall be intimately acquainted with the structural characteristics of the inner surface of the hock joint and know exactly where the site of spavin enlargement will be located.

To examine a hock one stands on the same side as the limb one intends to palpate, facing the animal's head. To palpate the left hock one uses the fingers of the right hand and to palpate the right hock the fingers of the left hand. It is technically incorrect to reverse this procedure and to stand facing the animal's tail.

The first landmark to identify is the internal malleolus of the tibia. Below this one comes to a projection which is the internal tuberosity of the astragalus, and immediately below this, a little anteriorly situated, is a rather flattened surface which overlies the rows of tarsal bones. This is the seat of spavin.

Below these again one will palpate the heads of the large and the inner small metatarsal bones. When one allows the tip of the second finger to travel gently (not forcefully) over the rows of flat bones it should be possible, at least in a thin-skinned animal, to feel the following grooves which indicate the spaces normally present between the bones:

(*a*) a transverse groove between the upper edge of the large metatarsal bone and the cuneiform magnum;

(*b*) a transverse groove between the cuneiform magnum and the scaphoid;

(*c*) a vertical groove between the large and small cuneiform bones. This lies above the groove between the heads of the large and small metatarsal bones, which can be clearly felt.

The student should procure a mounted specimen of the hockbones, including the lower end of the tibia and the upper ends of the three metatarsal bones, and compare this with the hock of the same side in the live horse, endeavouring by the aid of the former to identify the grooves in the latter. The importance of this is that in cases of spavin these grooves become filled with bony deposit and obliterated. The inability to detect the presence of well-defined grooves will point therefore to the presence of spavin. In addition, in arthritic conditions of the hock the calcareous outgrowths may extend on to the transverse ridges of the flat bones and produce flattened enlargements underlying the ligaments which cover the hock bones, or in some cases may protrude between them. Occasionally a spavin is represented by a comparatively large swelling, easily visible when one looks between the two forelimbs at the outline of the internal surfaces of the two hocks, but in the majority of cases presented for examination the swelling will be comparatively small and there may be some reasonable difficulty in identifying it with certainty without a deal of practice.

In draught horses and others possessing coarse skins and a thick subcutaneous fascia, it may be less easy to delineate the grooves lying between the bones. One then endeavours to detect any exostosis present by:

(a) Studying the contour of the inner aspect of each hock from the front, and also from the back, by holding aside the tail and "squinting" down between the two hocks. The animal must be standing perfectly squarely with the weight on all four feet.

(b) Palpating the antero-medial surface of each hock, stroking the site of spavin very gently with the finger tip, then comparing the "feel" of each hock in turn. Any obvious exostosis should be discovered. It must be remembered that both hocks may be equally enlarged and both affected with spavin.

There are two more features of spavin which may provide assistance:

(*a*) If the shoes are not new, the toe of the shoe of a "spavined" leg almost always shows excessive wear.

(*b*) If the foot is lifted from the ground and the hock fully flexed and held in this position for from sixty to ninety seconds and then released, the horse, led away immediately, will often show signs of impaired hock flexion and lameness may occur during a few steps, after which it disappears. This test is not entirely reliable, as other conditions than spavin may produce a similar reaction, especially in heavy horses and in aged, sound horses of any breed.

It is much more likely to pick out a shiverer, which when treated in this fashion will often tend to overbalance from a spasmodic over-flexion of the stifle and hock.

When a horse, lame from spavin, is trotted past one and back again, one will observe a lessening of hock flexion on the affected side. This is shown when the cap of one hock is not raised as high as that of the other hock, the lower being the one affected. When both hocks are spavined, the degree of flexion in each may match, and the lameness may be less evident than when only one hock is involved.

If the degree of flexion in one hock is exaggerated one must be on guard against stringhalt, and one must be careful not to regard a limb mildly affected with stringhalt as being normal and the sound limb as being limited in its flexion by the probable presence of a spavin. This is a mistake which has been recorded on more than one occasion.

An exostosis on the external inferior aspect of the hock joint is not uncommon. It may proceed from the lower row of tarsal bones and the head of the outer small metatarsal bone. In the majority of cases it does not cause permanent lameness.

Examination for the presence of a curb should first be made by taking up a position on one side of the hind limb, facing the external surface of the hock. One then views the contour of the posterior edge of the hock from its point downwards. In a normal hock, with the horse standing squarely, this posterior edge is perfectly perpendicular and straight throughout its length. It follows a line drawn from the tuber ischii at right angles to the ground beneath.

The second stage of the examination verifies this visual impression by following the line of the posterior edge of the hock with the tip of the second finger, feeling very carefully for any bulging of its surface or underlying fibrosis.

In so-called "curby hocks" the tuber calcis, instead of being upright, leans forward, probably as the result of a badly developed scaphoid. Accordingly, the hind limb from thigh to ground follows a slight curve, the concavity being formed at the front of the hock. This condition is akin to "sickle-hocks".

True curb, a strain of the calcaneo-metatarsal ligament, is shown by the presence of a convexity between the posterior edge of the tuber calcis and the head of the large metatarsal bone. The ligament feels hard and rather irregular, with a noticeable bulging down its hinder edge.

"False curb", often confused with true curb, is caused by a large, or enlarged, head of the small outer metatarsal bone. It must be remembered, however, that the calcaneo-metatarsal ligament is partially inserted into the head of the outer small metatarsal bone, so that in true curb a swelling is also noticeable over this area.

Curb will frequently cause lameness when the strain first appears, but later, when fibrosis of the ligament has become established, the lameness may disappear, although the thickening of the ligament usually persists. It may reappear after a hard day's hunting and again disappear after a few days' rest.

Curb is a definite unsoundness.

The examination of the remainder of the hind limb

follows the same lines as that described in the case of the forelimb.

The sole of the hind foot is more concave and the heels are usually better marked. This foot seldom suffers from navicular disease, corns, laminitis, or picked-up nails. Sidebone in a hind foot is a rarity. Ringbone may occasionally be encountered in a hind pastern or coronet. Canker and thrush are found in a hind perhaps more frequently than in a forefoot. Sandcrack at the toe is by no means infrequently encountered.

The tendons at the back of the metatarsal bones may occasionally become strained and fibrosed, but not nearly so frequently as in the forelimbs.

The skin of the hinder portion of the cannon may be affected with dermatitis (grease) or with leg mange, while the hinder parts of the pasterns may develop transverse fissures, as also occur in the forelegs. These frequently cause lameness (cracked heels).

The hind shoes may convey a deal of information according to the manner in which they become worn. Wearing of the toe is suggestive of spavin or of contracted tendons, but it may also arise from the wearing of calkins, as well as in draught horses in hilly regions, as in negotiating these the toe of the shoe slides, when the horse is endeavouring to hold back a load.

Examination of the Eye of the Horse

A preliminary inspection was made at the commencement of the examination, and a further detailed examination will be made when the horse returns to its box after the wind has been tested. The pupils will be sufficiently dilated at this time, and no mydriatic is employed.

The ophthalmoscope provides the best means of examination of the corneal surface, the lens and the fundus of the eye, with its optic disc and retinal vessels.

There are certain difficulties associated with the detailed ophthalmoscopic examination of the horse's eye, but for the purpose of detecting an opacity of the cornea or lens these are not of great importance.

The first difficulty may arise if the horse is not agreeable to having even a small light shone into the depths of its eye from short range, and some horses are apt to attempt to bite, or strike out with their forefeet. This applies when the electric, battery-type, ophthalmoscope is used. This risk is lessened and one stands farther away from the horse, if one uses a concave mirror fitted with a central diaphragm or peephole, and a light is arranged or a window is situated over and behind the animal's head. A lens of suitable strength (about $+15D$) may be made use of, held between the mirror and the eye of the horse at a convenient distance from the eye of the operator. The image seen is an inverted one. The usual distance between the eye of the patient and the observer is in this case 60 cm. The focus is corrected by moving the lens backwards, forwards, and to one or other side.

With a quiet animal, the electric ophthalmoscope is easier to manipulate. The second difficulty lies in the fact that all veterinary surgeons are not cast in the same mould and range from about 5 to $6\frac{1}{2}$ ft. in height. The result is that the two extremes view the eye from a different angle, the one looking upwards into it and the other downwards. When determining whether a horse is myopic this provides some difficulties. When making an examination to determine the degree of myopia or hypermetropia present, one uses the electric ophthalmoscope fitted with a number of graduated lenses, which may be rotated in succession. Each varies from the next by $0.5D$ or $1D$. On one side of the dial all the lenses are lettered plus (red) and on the other side minus (white). Briefly stated, the observer starting at $+0.5D$ revolves the lenses until the fundus of the eye and its blood vessels can be clearly focused. The reading of the number of the eyepiece is taken. One then has to make allowances for one's own eyesight if the examination is made by a person who normally wears glasses but has discarded them during the ophthalmoscopic examination. If he, himself, has a positive hypermetropia of $5D$ he may, if he wishes, commence by setting his instrument at $+5$ and subsequently add or subtract the additional diopters observed in the eyes of the horse. In actual practice a little additional adjustment has to be made to obtain accuracy, by mathematical formula in this way:

$$H \text{ (degree of hypermetropia)} = \frac{1}{D - d}$$

where D equals the focal length of the correcting glass and d equals distance from lens to cornea. So, if the graduated lens which gives the best view of the fundus is $2D$, this is equivalent to a focal length of 0·5 metre, as a diopter ($1D$) has a focal length of one metre, so:

$$H = \frac{1}{0 \cdot 5 - 0 \cdot 05} \text{ (the distance being measured at 5 cm.)}$$
$$= 2 \cdot 22D$$

The same method may show the presence of myopia. If at 10 cm. a glass, $-4D$, gives the clearest view of the depths of the eye, then:

$$M = \frac{1}{0 \cdot 25 + 0 \cdot 1} = \frac{1}{0 \cdot 26} = 3 \cdot 33D \text{ of myopia.}$$

In the horse the height of the observer, and accordingly his viewpoint, makes a great difference to the result, as the fundus of the horse is not round but "ramped", that is to say, the distance from the centre of the cornea to various parts of the retina varies, for it is largely by raising or lowering the head and allowing light rays to fall upon a different part of the retina that the horse focuses a distant object.

The rule therefore is that whatever the height of the observer, the observation with the ophthalmoscope is always made at the junction of the tapetum lucidum with the tapetum nigrum. This involves looking downwards into the eyeball through the pupil, and necessitates the short man standing upon a box or stool until his own eyes are raised a little above the level of the horse's eyes, while the tall man stoops.

To determine whether a horse is myopic, accurate measurement of the number of diopters can be dispensed with, provided that the examiner knows or estimates by means of the ophthalmoscope the condition of his own vision and makes the necessary correction on account of it. Approximately (only) it may then be reckoned in a rather rough-and-ready fashion that the horse registers either + degrees of hypermetropia or − degrees of myopia.

A horse with normal vision usually registers in the neighbourhood of roughly $0.5D$ to $1.5D$ of hypermetropia at the junction of the tapetum lucidum and tapetum nigrum, but if the reading is made elsewhere various fictitious results will be recorded from the same eye, usually on the minus (myopic) side of the scale.

A truly myopic horse can be a danger, especially over rough country. At one time it was believed that the majority of horses were myopic, but this was before it was realised that variations in reading depended more upon the height of the observer than upon the retina of the horse. It is probable that approximately 5–10 per cent of all horses are myopic.

For the detection of corneal opacities the eyepiece of the electric ophthalmoscope is set at about 15–20+, according to the vision of the observer, and adjusted until the best view of the corneal surface is obtained. To view the lens the eyepiece is set at 0.5 and then moved on to $1D$, $2D$, and so on, or set at $0.5-$, $0.1-$ until the light passes through the lens and gives a view of the depths of the fundus, the optic disc (low down in the fundus), and the tapetum lucidum. Any opacities, within or upon the lens, should now become visible as dull, or grey, areas through which the light fails to pass.

The older catoptric test is now rapidly passing out of use. In this, one observed the eye by the light of a candle in a darkened stable. The reflection of the light upon the cornea was upright; upon the front of the lens it was also upright, but upon the back of the lens it was inverted. By moving the light gently and slowly from side to side, any opacities upon the cornea, or on or within the lens, cut out the light falling upon one or other of the three surfaces.

The oblique method of illumination, using a shielded or "slit" torch to cast a beam upon the eye laterally or obliquely, gives a great deal of assistance at times in the detection of corneal opacities, and it may help to show up some lens opacities, but it is not so reliable as the ophthalmoscope.

To detect any corneal abrasions or ulceration, 1 per cent fluorescein solution may be instilled into the conjunctival sac. Where there is loss of surface tissue the cornea is stained yellow for a short time. The permission of the owner should first be obtained.

All opacities of the cornea and lens are regarded as unsoundness. Some doubt exists, nevertheless, as to whether small opacities of the cornea possess the degree of importance usually attributed to them. Probably this depends largely upon their position.

Examination for the Wind

The majority of adult light horses can be ridden if a rider is available. Heavy horses and colts and fillies of all ages are usually tested on a lungeing-rein. In the latter case it is essential that a safe and strong bridle or head collar shall be fitted so that there is no risk of the animal breaking loose. To this a rope of at least 15 yards in length is attached in such a way that it will not drag off the headgear if the animal stops and commences to go into reverse.

The animal is taken out into an open field or paddock free from obstacles, preferably on a non-slippery surface (difficult to guarantee the year round), and is first made to walk in a circle. The pace is gradually increased until a canter can be maintained. The direction, at first, should be anti-clockwise, but nearing the completion of the test it is well to change the direction for a few rounds.

There is not the least doubt that when the veterinary surgeon happens to be a competent rider, tests for wind are best made from the saddle, but this applies only to made horses and not to awkward animals, which can be handled better on a lungeing-rein. The legal responsibility incurred in riding other people's horses, as well as the question of whether the veterinary surgeon is covered under his normal accident policy as regards such risks, must also be taken into consideration. Moreover, every veterinary surgeon is not an expert equestrian. In this case it is necessary that any riding should be done by the owner or one of his representatives, and here other difficulties may arise. The writer, who earlier in life used always to ride his horses, later began to wonder whether the greater risk was on the back of the horse or in the centre of the field.

When the owner rides it is a good policy to select the smallest field possible, and the largest when one is doing the riding personally. Experienced dealers, given a large field where they can keep well out of hearing distance and choose their own pace, may be expert at disguising or concealing the noise a horse would make if ridden in a comparatively small circle. The veterinary surgeon will be wise if at the termination of an exhibition of this kind he insists on a final circle at a canter in each direction while he stands in the centre.

The noises which may proceed from a horse may be

F

normal sounds of respiratory distress, and one must learn to distinguish these from those arising from laryngeal or pulmonary disorder, e.g., *whistling*, *roaring*, and *emphysema*. Every horse, especially if fat or in soft condition, perhaps just off grass, may make a great deal of noise which may be no indication of unsoundness.

Highblowing is a sound not at all uncommon in fresh or excitable horses when taken from a roadway into a field and suddenly asked to gallop. The sounds associated with respiratory distress and highblowing are *expiratory* in origin, while whistling and roaring are almost always *inspiratory*, and dependent upon failure of air to pass through the larynx at a rapid pace without interference.

Grunting arises from a sudden forced expiration, such as occurs when a horse is threatened with a stick, especially in the region of his solar plexus (ribs or belly). Many horses grunt habitually when taking a jump, rolling on the ground, or when starting a load on a hill.

It is asserted by many observers that animals which have successfully passed through a roaring operation (stripping of the mucous membrane of the ventricle) will subsequently grunt when threatened with a stick, and that all horses affected with roaring or whistling in any marked degree do likewise. The writer has, probably in company with many others, encountered horses which grunted habitually to the stick but showed no observable indication of unsoundness when galloped.

One would be very rash in turning down a horse for wind merely because it grunted to the stick, without further proof. It must be remembered in all matters of examination for soundness it is as culpable to turn down a sound horse as to pass an unsound one.

The causation of whistling and roaring is similar. Any difference between the sounds heard depends upon a modification of the vibrations arising from variation in the tension of the vocal chords, and the degree of paralysis of the arytenoid cartilage.

As has already been mentioned, both these sounds arise during inspiration and are dependent upon partial obstruction of the entrance to the glottis by passive movements of the arytenoid cartilage or cartilages, or by some paralytic condition of the laryngeal muscles. Since the roaring operation has become popular, it has been noticed on several occasions during the actual operation that some horses which "make a noise" show no apparent changes in the motility of the cartilages.

Both roaring and whistling, the latter particularly, vary in intensity from time to time, apparently as the result of varying bodily fatness and muscular condition, and undoubtedly also according to the state of the weather and the degree of humidity. But, when these variations are well marked in the same individual, one must be particularly careful in making a diagnosis. The two other conditions one may have to distinguish are pharyngeal or nasal polypus, and intermittent paralysis of the soft palate, the latter of which may be allergic in nature.

The majority of whistlers in light breeds show signs before they reach seven years of age, although they may in rare cases develop the condition at a later age. A far greater proportion of heavy horses, particularly stallions, which have successfully passed their tests earlier in life will make a sound indistinguishable from roaring if violently exerted after they have obtained greater age. It must also be remembered that these animals are also in soft condition and may be overfat. One also runs some slight risk of heart failure when lungeing an aged stallion in fat and obviously unworkable condition.

Whistlers often develop later into roarers, or may continue to whistle throughout their lives, sometimes with very little diminution of their usefulness. Roarers rarely, if ever, become whistlers.

Wheezing is common in old, overfed horses, as well as in those affected with emphysema and a "broken-winded cough". Emphysema or broken wind will probably have been diagnosed during the preliminary examination when the breathing was noted at the flanks. It will be recognised, in company with other signs of distress, by the double expiratory movement of the flanks after the gallop. A short, barking cough should always cause one to suspect the existence of pulmonary emphysema, and after the exertion of the gallop auscultation of the chest will confirm it, the number of loud extraneous noises audible being positively alarming. Asthmatical and emphysematous conditions may nevertheless present a problem, as they vary in intensity and sometimes seem to disappear in mild cases according to varying factors, chief of which are the state of bodily condition and fatness, and the nature of the diet at the time. Dyspnœa due to œdema of the soft palate, may occur in an affected horse only a few times during the course of a hunting season, or it may be permanent when the paralysis depends upon nerve injury.

As soon as the horse has been brought to a standstill at the end of the gallop one should step forward, take hold of the bridle, and force the animal backward a few steps. This often serves to increase any sound which may have given rise to suspicion. Sometimes momentarily obstructing one nostril by pressure upon the wing of the nostril and then upon the other in turn may be helpful.

As soon as the rider has dismounted raise the head of the horse a little by placing the palm of the hand below the chin, and notice if the animal exhibits any signs of dizziness or staggering.

After the horse has calmed down a little the heart should again be carefully auscultated, any adventitious sounds noted and especially any tendency to intermittency or to double systole. The rate of the pulse should be checked as well as the respiration and five minutes and ten minutes later this should be done again and the recovery rate noted.

The horse should now be returned to its box and the ophthalmoscope used while the pupils are still widely dilated to examine the depths of the eye, especially for cataract.

After this has been done, the box door should be shut and the horse left entirely alone for at least a quarter of an hour or longer, if it can be made convenient. After this rest period the horse should be walked out of the box, then gently trotted up and down once more to ensure that no sign of lameness appears after a rest following forced exertion.

The Examination of Stallions

Veterinary surgeons are appointed by the Ministry of Agriculture, Fisheries and Food to examine stallions, prior to registration, under the Horse Breeding Act of 1918 and 1948.

This is a very onerous task, for not only is the veterinary surgeon responsible to the Ministry for the correctness of his report, but also to the horse-breeding community for the soundness of the stock the stallions will produce.

In addition to making out a certificate of soundness, the veterinary surgeon is required to fill in a form giving his opinion regarding the conformation of the animal, and this opinion is considered in conjunction with that of the Livestock Officer who also examines each horse entered for registration as regards its conformation and fitness to represent its breed.

The points stressed are those concerned with the possibility of handing down any varieties of hereditary unsoundness to the progeny, and a list of these is contained in the form of certificate supplied to the veterinary surgeon.

The method of examination is similar to that used in the examination of horses for purchase, but special attention is paid to the genital region, the wind, coronets, and hocks. The eyes, too, require very close examination with the ophthalmoscope, and the mouth must be carefully examined lest an overshot or undershot jaw be overlooked.

Testing stallions for their wind is sometimes rather difficult, either on account of their age, the fact that they must be circled on a lungeing rein, or because at the time at which examination is demanded fields are apt to be very slippery. In frosty weather it is best to defer examination as one runs a serious risk of throwing a horse, especially an aged one, and perhaps breaking a limb.

A list of the diseases and defects regarded as hereditary is given on page 8.

The Examination of Yearlings

Annual sales of yearlings are commonly organised by breeders of thoroughbreds in particular, while six-monthly or annual sales of ponies from the moors and from breeding establishments are now quite usual.

Most of the defects one may detect in young colts and fillies are congenital or at least hereditary, apart from those which arise from accident. The former include certain eye defects—entropion, dermoids, opacities of cornea or lens, and wall eyes or incomplete pigmentation of the iris. The two latter characteristics are usually included in identification. Jaw defects, overshot knees, bowed legs, sickle hocks, or congenital defects, such as umbilical or scrotal hernia, may be discoverable in odd cases.

A little difficulty may arise as regards testicular descent. Not every colt, which later may be quite sound, has both testicles down in the scrotum as a yearling, and in chilly weather they may be drawn up into the canal in any case. After a little exercise they should appear. Most yearling Thoroughbreds lead quite well on a head-collar, but few moorland ponies can be approached with any degree of safety in order to make a detailed examination of the genital region. Whenever one runs up against insuperable difficulties of this sort it is wise to mention in the certificate that examination for certain defects, or the examination of certain parts of the body which should be named, has been omitted.

It is also unwise, at any age, as has been shown in a number of Court cases, for the veterinary surgeon to include in his certificate such statements as "the owner guarantees (or warrants) the wind". It is better to state that this could not be examined at the time for a specified reason and accept no responsibility in connection with this particular feature.

The Examination of Mares with Foal

In such instances the certificate will include both animals, but each should be described and discussed separately.

The mare will be examined quite thoroughly as described in earlier pages and if the foal is of recent birth special attention will be paid to the mare's udder and teats, her vulva, vagina, and her perineum.

The condition of the vaginal mucous membrane will easily be determined by drawing back the lip of the vulva, while the perineum will be examined for signs of tearing or of suturing, past or present. The udder should be palpated and a little milk drawn from each teat. The demeanour of the mare towards her foal will be observed, and it will be noted whether the foal is sucking normally.

If the foal is newly-born it may be advisable to ascertain by inquiry and observation if the afterbirth has been completely cast. One will see that the foal is passing meconium normally and that no milk escapes down its nostrils when it attempts to suck (cleft palate).

The foal should be examined also for signs of any jaw

abnormality, and for umbilical or scrotal hernia. Its fore-limbs may be bent at the knees and/or fetlocks from con-tracted tendons, or it may be bowlegged or calf-kneed. Its anus should be examined if it has not passed meconium to assure oneself that there is no evidence of it being imper-forate. Any dripping of urine from the umbilicus will be carefully noted.

In a foal aged a week to a fortnight, the ruptured end of the umbilical cord should have withered away and the umbilicus should be healed and dry. The foal will be active and sucking at frequent intervals; its joints will appear normal, with no evidence of lameness or swelling. Any marked abnormality of conformation should be entered in the certificate. Features such as a Roman nose, or a wall eye, should be entered in the identification. Entropion is not rare in foals, and this should be carefully noted, for if attention is not drawn to it the foal may become blind.

Horses for Export

Horses examined for export may be travelling to another country to a purchaser who intends to work them, race them, or breed from them, or they may be consigned to another country for purpose of slaughter. The law relating to the export of horses should be studied in the appropriate volumes.

The examination will in all probability be concerned only with the fitness or otherwise of the animal to travel without being subjected to undue suffering, and does not normally include an examination to decide whether the animal is workably sound. Marked lameness or inability to lie and rise, obvious illness or debility, the presence of wounds, neoplasms, or of any impediment to easy respiration, will rank among some of the reasons for refusal of a certificate. The animal should be in sufficiently good condition to enable it to keep its feet on a rolling vessel.

Any very obvious unsoundnesses which do not interfere with the ability to travel safely should be entered in the identification chart of the animal. A very detailed description should accompany the horse so that there can be no grounds for mistaken identity or substitution, or for the certificate being used for a somewhat similar animal. It is advisable in parti-coloured animals that all markings should be drawn on a diagram.

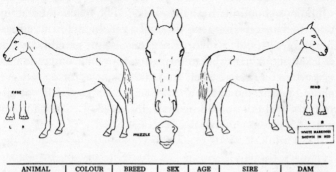

ANIMAL	COLOUR	BREED	SEX	AGE	SIRE	DAM

MARKINGS
- **HEAD:**
- **LIMBS:**
- **BODY:** (Including Height)
- **ACQUIRED:**
- **REMARKS:**

Date...........................

ADDRESS:...............................   ...........................R.C.V.S.

The Veterinary Certificate

One must exercise great care in writing a certificate. The animal must be described in such a way that there can be no possibility of mistake in its identity. When a horse has few characteristics which will ensure its recognition, endeavour to discover at least one or two features which will assist and make it less easy to substitute one horse for another. A drawing of white marks, hair whorls, giving colour of feet and other salient features, in addition to a recording of the age and exact height, may be made on one of the printed certificate forms recommended by the Sub-Committee of the Royal College of Veterinary Surgeons.*

The Sub-Committee also recommended, as mentioned on page 19, that in making out the certificate the following order should be adopted: Colour, Breed, Sex, Age, Height; marks on head (including eyes) in the order described above; marks on limbs; fore first, then hind, commencing from below; marks on body, including mane and tail; acquired marks, congenital abnormalities, whorls, or any other features of note.

In addition, the certificate will contain the address of the veterinary surgeon carrying out the examination, his signature, and the date.

One will pay particular attention to the recording of any unusual markings or features, such as wall eyes, lack of pigmentation in or surrounding the eyelids, flesh marks, scars, superficial enlargements, and the colour of the feet. The name of the animal is best omitted unless it happens to be a registered stallion or an animal well known to the veterinary surgeon. The late Professor Macqueen, of the London Veterinary College, used the following form of certificate for thirty years:

* A specimen copy of the suggested certificate is appended. It is obtainable from H. R. Grubb, Ltd., Poplar Walk, Croydon, Surrey.

CERTIFICATE OF EXAMINATION AS TO SOUNDNESS

Date:......... No.:.........   No.   Address: ....

For..............................   I certify that I have this day examined

....   at the request of ....

   the following animal ....

	Colour and Sex:	Age:	Height:	Distinguishing Marks:
Colour and Sex:				

Age: ....

Height: ....

Marks: ....

Opinion: ....   The said animal is in my opinion ......

....

Defects: ....   Defects: ....

   ....

(Initials)   Date   Date:.........   Signature:...............

       Signature:

Following are two typical examples of certificates as issued by a practising veterinary surgeon. They are typed on headed notepaper.

(I)   Address.

                      Date.

I certify that I have this day examined at the request of Mr. Y. of —— at his Burleybridge Stables, the following animal: Brown, heavyweight hunter gelding, 7 years, 16·3 h.h. with small triangular star and narrow stripe extending to between nostrils. Flesh mark in shape of an inverted V on upper lip. Muzzle black.

There is a narrow, white linear longitudinal marking, six

inches in length, immediately behind the umbilicus in the mid-line of the belly.

Right fore fetlock white, extending down front of coronet with black heel. There is a scar, two inches by one inch in the skin of the outer side of the left forearm. Both hind limbs black from immediately above feet to hocks.

I found a slight, fibrous enlargement, superficially placed, on the outer side of the left fore fetlock. The wall of the right hind foot was somewhat broken, probably the result of casting a shoe. I was unable to find any unsoundness, and with the exception of the defects mentioned I am of opinion that at the time of my examination the gelding was sound.

Signed: ....

(II)   Address.

                                  Date.

I certify that I have this day examined at his own premises, at the request of Mr. Y. of —— the following animal: Blue roan hackney mare, 10 years, 15·1 h.h. Roan face, white upper lip and white between lower jaws extending over lower lip. There is an absence of pigmentation of the right upper eyelid and a similar lack in the nasal segment of the iris of the right eye.

There is a small, circular black patch immediately behind the left wither. Left forelimb white from foot to knee, other limbs blue roan, rather darker than the general body colour. The left and both hind feet are black, the right forefoot white.

I found a narrow linear opacity crossing the cornea of the right eye.

I also found a small spavin on the left hock which interferes with full hock flexion and causes slight lameness, which disappears on exercise.

In my opinion the mare was unsound at the time of my examination.

Signed: ....

General Considerations Concerning the Examination of Horses for Soundness

The veterinary surgeon examining the horse is responsible only to the person who employs him. His findings and his report to his client are entirely confidential, and not to be disclosed by the veterinary surgeon to any person other than the one by whom he is employed.

There are one or two conditions which may be entitled to a little further consideration.

Young horses go lame so frequently from splints that one may have to decide how much importance should be attributed to a small splint in a three-year-old, intended for hunting in a year or two. Certainly, the defect must be recorded in the certificate, as the animal was unsound at the time of examination. But in such a case a great deal depends on the animal's conformation. If this is a weedy animal with light bone, an upright shoulder, and a short, erect pastern, the possibility is that the splint may cause intermittent lameness for some time. But if the horse has good bone, short cannons, good shoulders and pasterns, the probability is that the lameness will soon disappear, and if no other unsoundness is present or develops the splint will not interfere with the usefulness of the animal once fusion between the large and small metacarpals has occurred. In such a case the writer would consider that the veterinary surgeon would be justified in explaining to his client if invited to express an opinion, that in all probability the present unsoundness, viz., the splint, may be of no great consequence in a few months' time, although at present it constitutes an unsoundness.

One cannot put up any good argument for a horse with a small spavin, but many horses with large, well-developed spavins do slow work comfortably for many years. Any degree of spavin is an unsoundness.

Some forms of unsoundness are not always in evidence,

they show a variable intermittency, and although one cannot be expected to discover a defect which is not evident, the veterinary surgeon should be aware of the possibility of certain defects appearing only upon occasion.

A horse may carry a pharyngeal or post-nasal polypus which does not interfere with hunting generally, but on occasion it may descend into the laryngeal region and cause immediate dyspnœa. If this is exhibited a week after purchase and the growth removed by operation, it will then be evident that the horse was unsound at the time of examination. Similarly, one occasionally encounters a horse which at times develops an œdema or a paralysis of the soft palate which may appear without warning and almost suffocate the animal. These attacks appear to result from a form of allergy. The veterinary surgeon might examine either of these animals on four days in any week and detect nothing abnormal. In either of the above cases the onus would fall upon the veterinary surgeon to prove that he made a competent examination and at that time the unsoundness could not have been detected.

Cough is also liable to be intermittent. Some horses kept at grass, and brought in from pasture for examination never cough, but do so continuously when stabled and fed hay. Others develop a "grass cough" and remain apparently normal while stabled.

Crib-biting usually leaves indications on the tables of the incisor teeth, as well as on the manger, but windsuckers may betray nothing when stirred up during an ordinary examination, but may perform regularly if put into harness or left in idleness.

Another animal to which one should pay particular attention is the horse brought off grass after a long rest. It is usually freshly shod, carries a rough coat in most cases, and shows no bridle or saddle marks. Such horses have sometimes been turned away on account of lameness, although a number of hunters may be presented for examination in early autumn which have grazed throughout the summer and may be quite sound.

A long experience of examining horses for soundness only confirms the fact that the more one knows about horses, and their owners, the more worrying a task examining horses can become. The writer has recollections of a very experienced veterinary surgeon, many years ago, who declared that whenever he passed a horse as sound he was unable to sleep at night through wondering whatever it could have been that he had overlooked!

Chapter Two

THE TEETH OF ANIMALS
AS A GUIDE TO AGE

THE contents of this chapter are not intended to be a treatise on the dentition of animals but to indicate a few of the more obvious characteristics of the teeth of various animals as an indication of their age.

All veterinary surgeons will have received instruction concerning dentition generally. Dentition as a guide to age can be accepted only within certain limits. It is not infallible. Animals differ in the nature of their teeth, the thickness of the enamel, and the hardness of the dentine, as much as in the nature of the food they eat and the water they drink. Horses which graze on very short pasture, particularly on granite soil, will wear down their teeth much more rapidly than those fed on a loam soil with richer foliage, and much faster than horses kept indoors and fed on crushed oats, bran, and hay.

The Teeth of the Horse

The horse, mule, and ass normally have six incisor teeth, consisting of two centrals, two laterals, and two corner teeth. *Although veterinary surgeons and horse owners almost invariably use this terminology, one may use the terms: first, second, and third pairs of incisors.* There are six cheek teeth on either side of each jaw, made up of three premolars and three molars. The three premolars become changed for permanent premolars.

The Foal

At birth: Two central incisors. These may not appear until the 7th or 10th day.

At 4–6 weeks: Lateral incisors appear.

At 6–9 months: Corner incisors appear.

At 1 year: All six temporary incisors are present but only the centrals show marked wear of their tables. Corners sharp and shell-like.

At 2 years: All incisors show wear of their tables. The infundibulum will have disappeared from centrals and laterals, possibly from the corners.

At $2\frac{1}{2}$ years: Central incisors loose or shed.

At 3 years: Two permanent centrals are up and in wear.

At $3\frac{1}{2}$ years: Temporary laterals shed.

At 4 years: Laterals in wear.

At $4\frac{1}{2}$ years: Corner temporary incisors shed.

At 5 years: Corner incisors in wear.

Both at 2 years and 5 years there will be a full set of incisors, temporary at 2 years, permanent at 5 years.

Temporary incisors appear rather fragile and shelly. They are smaller than permanent incisors. Their biting edges tend to curl over like the edges of a shell and they are pear-shaped, with the waisted part next the gum. At 1 year old the temporary incisors are close together, but at 2 years the jaw has widened and there may be slight gaps between the teeth, especially near the gums.

On a great many occasions 2-year-olds have been mistaken for 5-year-olds, and vice versa.

A 2-year-old housed, fed, and groomed, may in appearance

G

resemble a 5-year-old externally on first sight, but to the practised eye the state of development and furnishing is usually more evident in the 5-year-old.

The tail of a 2-year-old is usually shorter than that of a 5-year-old, reaching to just above or level with the hocks. In a 5-year-old it usually reaches to well below the hocks. Even this is a variable feature and, in any case, tails may be pulled or trimmed. Tail length is often a useful guide in moorland ponies running out. Tails are also apt to grow faster with good feeding and housing.

If any real doubt is experienced, the solution lies in an examination of the cheek teeth.

At birth the foal carries *three* cheek teeth; all temporary premolars which later will be cast and exchanged for permanent premolars.

At *1 year old* it has *four* cheek teeth; the three premolars and the first permanent molar.

At *2 years old* the colt or filly has *five* cheek teeth; three premolars and the first and second molars.

At *4–5 years old* it has *six* cheek teeth; three permanent premolars and all three molars.

A supernumerary premolar, the so-called Wolf tooth, may appear in front of the first premolar, at 5–6 months.

That in the upper jaw is usually shed. In the lower jaw it often persists.

The Tushes or Canine teeth are usually present only in the male, though small rudimentary tushes are quite common in the female. These appear at $3\frac{1}{2}$–4 years and are fully developed at $4\frac{1}{2}$–5 years. *They will be absent in a 2-year-old.* At first they are grooved on their inner surfaces, but this groove has worn away by the 7th year.

The age of horses from 5 years upwards is not so easy to judge accurately. The incisors at 6 years meet at a right angle in a well-formed mouth, with no forward inclination. After this age they commence to incline in a forward direction progressively with the years, until at 20 years they meet at an acute angle, while at 25–30 they are almost horizontally placed.

The tables of the incisors serve as a guide from 6 years onwards. After 7–8 years a horse is somewhat unjustly referred to as "aged".

Each permanent incisor carries on its table a dark, depressed ring known as the "infundibulum". The dark ring is surrounded by a light coloured ring of enamel.

At 6 years: The infundibulum has worn away, but a trace of enamel may remain.

At 7 years: The infundibulum has disappeared from the centrals and laterals, apart from a trace of enamel.

At 8 years: The infundibulum has disappeared from *all* the incisors.

Later, due to wearing away of the crowns of the incisor teeth, a central mark appears in the tables owing to exposure of the pulp cavity. The time of its appearance is a little variable and will depend upon feeding conditions and the quality of the teeth.

Usually at 8 years it appears in the central incisors.

Usually at 9 years it appears in the lateral incisors.

Usually at 10–12 it is present in all the incisors.

The shape of the tables varies from oval to triangular and then to round as the horse becomes older.

In the horse up to 7 years—oval tables.

In the horse at 9 years—centrals triangular.

In the horse at 10 years—laterals triangular.

In the horse at 11 years—corners triangular.

After 13 years the tables become rounded with a central pulp mark.

At an advanced age the tables again become oval, but this time from front to back.

The Notch or Hook

The corner incisor tooth does not wear evenly throughout its length, so that a projection or hook develops at its hinder edge, and as the tooth wears from front to back without reducing the length of the hook, one gets the impression that the tooth carries a projection downwards from its rear edge. This hook and accompanying notch first appear at 7 years.

At 8 years the hook has worn away somewhat, and by 8½–9 years the incisor surface is again level.

At 11 years the hook reappears and the notch becomes successively deeper, so that by 13 years it is very noticeable. After this it usually persists throughout life.

Galvayne's Groove

This is a well-marked longitudinal groove which first appears as a notch at the outer side of each upper corner tooth just below the gum. As the animal ages it travels down the tooth as a narrow longitudinal furrow, often stained yellow or brown.

It makes its appearance at 10 years; in occasional cases, rather earlier.

It has reached half-way down the tooth at 15 years.

It has reached the bottom of the tooth at 20 years.

At 25 years it has disappeared from the upper half of the tooth.

At 30 years it has disappeared completely.

The Teeth of the Ox

There are no incisors in the upper jaw. Those in the lower jaw are slightly movable in a forward direction. The place of the upper incisors is taken by the hard dental pad and the length of the jaws must correspond so that the edges of the incisor teeth do not cut into the pad but reach its anterior aspect in order that the teeth when protruding forward under pressure shall overlap the dental pad by only a very small fraction of an inch.

The bovine incisors have not flat tables and an infundibulum as in the horse, but are chisel shaped.

According to their breed and the length of time they have been carried in utero, calves may be born with only four temporary incisors or the complete eight. When only four are present at birth the remaining four appear within the next 3–4 weeks. Their incisors are described as centrals, middles, laterals, and corners. The temporary teeth are all of small size and possess very definite necks. Some authorities refer to these teeth as the first, second, third, and fourth pairs of incisors.

The cheek teeth, whether premolars (3) or molars (3), are also more or less chisel-shaped but have well-formed grinding surfaces. Owing to the habit of rumination, the cheek teeth cross each other either from inside to outside or vice versa at regular intervals, being capable of grinding in either direction.

At birth the calf has 4–8 incisors.

At 1 year 9 months the permanent centrals are cut and are in wear at 2 years old.

At 2 years the ox has therefore 2 permanent *central* incisors in wear with the middle temporary teeth firmly in position (1st pair).

At 2 years 3 months the temporary *middle* incisors are replaced by permanent teeth which are in wear by 2 years 6 months (2nd pair).

At 2 years 9 months the temporary *laterals* are cast and the permanents which replace them are in wear by 3 years (3rd pair).

At 3 years 3 months the *corners* are cut and all the permanent incisors are in wear by 3 years 6 months (4th pair).

When, as occasionally happens, an animal believed to be

only 3 years has a full mouth of 8 permanent incisors, reference may be made to the 3rd premolar. If this tooth has been replaced by a permanent tooth which is engaging the opposite tooth, the animal is fully 3 years old.

The fourth cheek tooth (first molar) appears at 6 months.

The fifth cheek tooth (second molar) appears at from 1 year to 1 year 3 months.

The sixth cheek tooth (third molar) appears at from 2 years to 2 years 3 months.

In cattle possessing natural horns (not scraped and polished for exhibition) some idea of the age can be obtained by counting the rings and adding two years. A cow possessing three well-defined rings should therefore be approximately 5 years old.

The first and second temporary premolars are changed at 2–2 years 3 months and the third at $2\frac{1}{2}$–3 years. It is by no means uncommon for the permanent tooth to become impacted in the shell of the temporary tooth. In examining heifers at about this age for purchase, it is always wise to check up on the cheek teeth in case this has occurred.

The Teeth of Sheep

In most cases the lamb is born without any temporary incisors. The centrals and middles are cut at about a week old, the laterals at 2 weeks, and the corners at a month.

The incisors are changed to permanent teeth as follows:

> Centrals—1 year 3 months, in wear at 1 year 6 months (1st pair).
>
> Middles—1 year 9 months, in wear at 2 years (2nd pair).
>
> Laterals—2 years 3 months, in wear at 2 years 6 months (3rd pair).
>
> Corners—2 years 9 months, to 3 years, in wear at 3 years–3 years 3 months (4th pair).

A 2-toothed sheep is approximately 18 months old.

A 4-toothed sheep is approximately 2 years old.

A 6-toothed sheep is approximately 2½ years old.

A "full-mouthed" sheep is 3 years old or over.

A "broken-mouthed" sheep is over 4 years old.

The incisor teeth become chipped and brown with age.

The cheek teeth are all cut and in wear by 2 years old.

The three temporary premolars are present at 2–4 weeks.

The three permanent molars appear at 3 months, 9–12 months, and 18 months, in that order.

The Teeth of the Pig

Veterinary surgeons are required to age pigs for purpose of exhibition. The pig has six incisors, two pairs of tushes, and six cheek teeth in each jaw.

At birth: there are present 2 pairs of temporary tushes and the corner temporary tooth (3rd incisor).

At 1 month: Central incisors appear (1st pair).

At 2 months: Lateral incisors appear (2nd pair).

At 9 months: *Permanent* corners (3rd pair of incisors) and *permanent* tushes appear.

At 12 months: Central *permanent* incisors appear (1st pair).

At 18 months: Lateral *permanent* incisors appear (2nd pair).

The second and third temporary premolars appear at 1 week after birth in the upper jaw; and at 3–4 weeks in the lower.

The first temporary premolars do not appear until 4–6 weeks.

The fourth cheek tooth (1st molar) appears at 5 months.

The fifth cheek tooth appears at 10 months.

The Teeth of the Dog

The dog possesses 28 temporary teeth and 42 or 44 permanent teeth.

The puppy is born toothless.

The temporary canines appear at 3–4 weeks and all six incisors are present at the 4th to 5th week.

At about 4 months the permanent central and lateral incisors first make an appearance.

At 4½–5 months the corners are changed.

The adult dog has 12 incisors, 4 canines, 16 premolars, and 10 molars. The teeth in the upper and lower jaw are not numerically equal. The permanent dental formula is

$$\text{I.T.P.M.}$$

$$\frac{3\ \ 1\ 4\ \ 2}{3\ \ 1\ 4\ \ 3}$$

The upper jaw carries only 2 molars, while the lower jaw carries 3 molars. The carnassial tooth, the largest tooth, is the 4th premolar of the upper jaw and it approximates with the 1st molar of the lower jaw, which is similarly shaped.

The 1st, 2nd, and 3rd premolars appear at about 3–4 weeks and are changed at between 5 and 6 months.

About this time the 5th cheek tooth (1st molar) appears in the upper jaw. The 6th cheek tooth (2nd molar) arrives in the lower jaw at 6–8 months. It is frequently absent from the upper jaw.

The fact that a dog possesses a complete set of permanent cheek teeth in the lower jaw, seven teeth on either side, indicates that it is at least 6 months old and eligible to possess a licence.

Chapter Three

THE EXAMINATION OF CATTLE

It has become an increasingly usual practice to submit cattle before purchase to veterinary examination for soundness. Pedigree and attested cattle now command very high prices, and although the demand for bulls may have lessened somewhat since the advent of artificial insemination, the supply of good calves, heifers, and in-calvers, as well as of heavy milkers, is hardly equal to the demand. Veterinary examination is frequently required in connection with private purchase and the disposal of pedigree cattle in farm or market auction sales, as well as with the purchase of calves from pedigree and commercial herds.

Young bulls are examined for purpose of licence or registration by livestock officers, and if the officer suspects that an animal, particularly a young bull, is in any way abnormal a veterinary surgeon is called upon to make a report to his Ministry. In the majority of cases the matter under consideration is in connection with the genital organs of the bull and the possibility of it transmitting hereditary defects or of being infertile.

Cattle are also examined prior to export, and in some cases the veterinary examination of animals intended for food is required prior to slaughter. It is probable that within a short time such examination will be generally demanded in order that this country may attain the standard of protection of public health insisted upon in other countries.

Cattle are also examined prior to insurance, and at most large exhibitions veterinary examination is required.

In other instances the veterinary examination of cattle may be confined to detection of the clinical signs of certain animal diseases, such as foot-and-mouth disease and tuberculosis.

The Examination of Dairy Cows

Frequently a private buyer wishes to purchase one or more recently calved cows to add to his existing herd or possibly as house cows, and he requires a veterinary certificate indicating that the animals are sound and apparently healthy. It will be necessary to ascertain whether the examination is required to cover physical soundness only, or whether it is desired that the animal or animals are to be declared free from tuberculosis, Johne's disease, brucella infection, and venereal diseases, such as trichomoniasis and vibrio infections. The majority of cows are now from attested herds or have been tuberculin-tested. The other diseases do not come within the scope of this volume.

The examination of a cow for soundness entails a great many observations, and although in many ways it differs from the examination of the horse, it is almost equally exacting, and unless one proceeds in a routine fashion certain types of unsoundness may easily be overlooked.

As in the horse, there must be a preliminary examination by general observation from a short distance away from the animal, to be followed by a more detailed examination by immediate contact.

One first views the animal generally, then the whole of the body from the four points; front, rear, and two sides. This is the best time, too, to record a full description of the cow, omitting no detail, however small, which will assist in identification. The breed, colour, and, so far as can be judged, the approximate age, together with all visible markings will be written down.

A printed diagram of each side of a cow's outline may be used to draw in the white marks and to locate any scars or blemishes. In cattle possessing horns, the shape, number of horn rings, and any difference in the direction or appearance of the two horns, as well as any minor blemishes, such as a tear in the lip of the vulva, horn scars, a scarred teat, a supernumerary teat, or any feature which strikes one at the time, may be included in the description.

During the superficial inspection which comes before the more detailed examination, one will first notice the general appearance of the cow, her bodily condition, the state of her coat and hide, and also that of her feet. One will take particular notice of the udder and teats of a newly calved cow. In heifers, particularly, a little œdema in front of the udder at this time will be attributed to natural causes. The cow should be of a good colour; a faded colour, brick-red for instance, in a cow normally of a bright or deep red, will raise suspicions as to the state of her health. If a fold of skin is raised from the ribs between finger and thumb, it should be loose and free, and when released it should immediately flatten itself out.

The coat should be smooth and glossy, and it should carry "lick-marks" to show that the cow is properly interested in her toilet. On the other hand, a rough coat in summer-time, with too many "lick marks", may raise a suspicion that the cow may be harbouring lice. Look carefully for any signs of ringworm on the face, eyelids, neck, or body and look also at the limbs for the presence of swellings caused by the so-called "skin tuberculosis".

Any roughness or irritation of the skin of the neck, back, or tail head may be further investigated in case it arises from the presence of parasitic mange.

Now observe the habits of the cow, whether she is placid, chewing her cud, or whether she is highly strung and excitable.

If she is outdoors at the time, notice how she crops grass, and how she chews it, and if she salivates unduly. If she feeds in a normal manner, does not salivate, and licks herself freely with normal protrusion of the tongue, it is at least unlikely that she will be suffering from either actinobacillosis or disorders of her cheek teeth. This need not preclude a more detailed examination later.

If the cow is ruminating, observe the number of bites she takes in one direction and those in the other direction, whether the cow belches normally as a cow should do; if there is any evidence of excessive rumenal tympany or, on the other hand, whether the triangle over the rumen appears hollow, as if the stomach were half-empty.

In a freshly calved cow look carefully for anything indicating retention of the whole or portion of the afterbirth. Notice whether milk is leaking, either dripping or running away from the teats, and if the calf happens to be with the cow observe whether it sucks freely, if it neglects any particular quarter, and how the cow behaves towards it.

The jugular vein may be watched to see if it shows undue venous pulsation (a very slight degree of pulsation in cattle is not always abnormal). Look at the submaxillary space and at the dewlap for any evidence of œdema or, alternatively, of bruising. Do not confuse either of these with the "solid" feeling presented by the dewlap of a fat cow, especially of a Shorthorn.

Notice the line of the back, whether it is perfectly straight as it should be, or if it is "roached" or "hollow" and dipped.

Look at the tail head and see if it follows the line of the back or whether it is very prominent and carried high, with an elevated tail and a hollow space on either side of it due to slackened pelvic ligaments. In a newly calved cow this may be quite normal, but after 48–60 hours, any prominence should have settled down to normal. When it does not do so shortly after calving it may be an indication of a low blood-calcium level, with a disposition towards milk fever. In a case of a "barren" cow, or of one which had calved several months, one might, in similar circumstances, suspect ovarian disorder, which could to some extent be decided if one could see the animal when turned out with other cows, when she might display signs of nymphomania.

Note the appearance of the tail and rump, whether it is clean and dry, or dirty and soiled with liquid fæces.

Look at the two haunch or pin-bones, see if they are perfectly level on either side, or if one has been "knocked down". At the same time observe any sign of hæmatoma of the pin-bone, or of the tuber ischii (seat bone), or flank. A very common place for an extensive hæmatoma, caused by a horn-gore is the flank, running alongside the base of the udder. While making this examination carefully note any tendency to cough. If a cough is present, observe the type of cough and its sound, whether it suggests hoose, emphysema, or tuberculosis.

During the detailed examination you will pay particular attention to the sounds proceeding from the thorax when you auscultate the lungs and heart. If you wish to hear a little more of the cough to determine its origin, you may gently squeeze the trachea, below the larynx, for a few seconds. You will also carefully examine the respiration of the flank and make a note of the pulse, temperature, and respiration rate.

If the cow appears to have been dehorned during the past few months, look at the scar and see if healing is complete, whether there are any signs of a purulent nasal discharge or of sinus infection.

In parti-coloured cattle, especially in Friesians, during hot, sunny weather, carefully palpate any white areas of skin on the shoulders, back, or rump, in case the cow exhibits any tendency to photo-sensitisation, with dermatitis of the white areas.

The detailed examination will commence at the head. Ears, horns, nose, mouth, and eyes will be inspected.

When horns are present be on the look out for a loose horn, a cracked or broken horn, one which has had its horny covering knocked off and quickly "replaced", and for horns which are growing inwards towards the eye. Be on guard against a unilateral facial paralysis with drooping of an eyelid, or of one side of a lip.

The eyes will need an examination, not perhaps quite so detailed as in the horse, but none the less important, since cattle have a number of eye conditions all their own. One of these is bulging of the eyeball from the orbit, which may be caused in several ways. In such conditions the eye may be distended with fluid (hydrophthalmos), or the eyeball may be normal apart from its position. Hydrophthalmos is the less-common condition, and may result from any disease (glaucoma) or injury which interferes with the rapid exchange of aqueous humour between the ciliary body and the lymph channels of the eyeball.

The causes of bulging or protrusion of the eyeball are: (a) thyroid abnormalities, such as exophthalmic goitre which is not uncommon among Jerseys; (b) strabismus, a more or less pronounced "squint", encountered in many breeds, notably Channel Island cattle and Shorthorns, in which the eyeball may be rotated to such an extent that only the sclera, the white portion, shows. Cases of marked strabismus are also commonly associated with hydrophthalmos which causes the protrusion.

In Jerseys and Guernseys blindness may occur at an early age, and it may persist throughout life, arising from pressure upon the optic nerve as the result of an imperfectly developed optic foramen. This condition is associated with avitaminosis A. There is commonly a certain amount of bulging of the eye, dilatation of the pupil, and an increasing loss of vision. Any protrusion of the membrana nictitans over the front of the eyeball may result from the presence of a foreign body beneath it, or free in the conjunctival sac. The common oat husk is an example, or it may arise from conjunctivitis due to irritant dust, or from contagious bovine conjunctivitis, or from contagious keratitis due to infection by *Morexella bovis*.

In addition, one must be on the look out for the occasional squamous-celled carcinoma of the orbit, which first appears in the membrana nictitans, or in the conjunctiva at the junction of the cornea and sclera. It may be quite small when first noticeable, slightly nodular, and highly vascular. It extends until it eventually causes a loss of the whole orbital content.

Tuberculosis of the eyeball in cattle attacks the iris and choroid. It may first appear as a liver-coloured projection, partly occluding the pupil. Amaurosis—blindness of uncertain origin—is by no means uncommon in cattle, particularly following parturition. Heifers, as well as cows, may go completely blind quite suddenly. The possible causes are quite numerous and varied.

Opacities of the cornea may result from the presence, past or present, of foreign bodies, or may be caused by horn gores or thorn punctures, or they may be left after an attack of contagious keratitis.

Cataract may be encountered, but it is not so commonly seen in cattle as in some other animals. It may be diagnosed, as in the horse, by using the black shield to cast a shadow upon the pupil, or by the ophthalmoscope. It is always wise to see a cow loose in a yard or field to discover if it can find its way readily between obstacles in its path.

The tongue is important, and it should be observed when one examines the teeth.

Broken or worn incisors must be recorded, as well as any evidence of tooth damage arising from fluorosis.

The relative length of the upper and lower jaws is nowadays regarded as of great importance, and great care is being taken when registering or licensing cattle, as well as in the judging ring, to discard any which show a tendency to either an overshot or undershot mouth.

It was mentioned in Chapter Two when discussing the teeth of cattle as a guide to age, that there are no upper incisors, their place being taken by the firm dental pad. It was never intended that the sharp chisel edges of the lower incisors should bite directly onto (or into) this pad. The lower incisors are not rigidly fixed, but have a little play in the forward direction, so that their edges should meet the anterior edge of the dental pad and then by their own freedom under pressure slide over its anterior border.

A lower jaw which is sufficiently short to enable the edges of the incisors to cut into the dental pad is unsound. Also is one which is sufficiently long to enable the edges of the incisors to pass completely in front of the dental pad, so that no use can be made of this structure.

Another defect of the bovine mouth which may fairly frequently be met with in cattle of all ages is the so-called "smooth mouth".

Normally there are large papilliform outgrowths, covered by mucous membrane, from the sides of the hinder portion of the tongue, and especially from the inside of each cheek.

Many of these are directed backward and prevent food escaping from the mouth, especially during rumination. Calves are sometimes born without these papillæ. The result is that calves and heifers accumulate masses of chewed material between the cheeks and the cheek teeth. Being unable to get rid of them, their food content becomes sour or putrid and in turn produces a sore mouth. These masses can be removed by the finger quite easily.

In the adult the absence of papillæ permits the escape of part of the cud. "Smooth mouth" must be classed as an unsoundness.

In cattle of from 2¼ to 3 years inability to feed freely may be due to impaction of the cheek teeth, the permanent pre-molar becoming impacted in the crown of the temporary tooth. This can be recognised if the teeth are examined with the aid of a torch while the tongue is held, or when a gag is applied.

The submaxillary glands of the whole body surface as well as those of the parotid region should be palpated, and anything in the nature of a "wen" should be noted. There should be no sign of œdema present in the submaxillary space or in the dewlap. If the dewlap appears to be very large one must distinguish between: (a) normal fatness in heavy breeds and in beef animals; (b) hæmatoma arising from bruising; (c) œdema due to cardiac disability or anæmia. In œdema associated with traumatic pericarditis, a jugular pulse will also be evident as well as abnormal heart sounds on auscultation.

An œdematous condition of the submaxillary space may be indicative of actinobacillosis, Johne's disease, parasitism or heart or blood disorders. The jugular furrow will be examined on either side to test its patency. This is done by checking the flow of blood momentarily with the thumb. One will also search for any indications of fibrosis or throm-bosis caused by the withdrawal of blood from the vein for diagnostic purposes or employment of the vein for the administration of intravenous injections. While occupied with veins, it is as well to pay a like attention to the two milk veins.

Hæmatoma may be the cause of swelling on any prominent portion of the body, particularly the angles of the haunch, seat bones, knees, and hocks, but a very common site is the subcutaneous tissue of the flank alongside the udder.

H

Damage to the subcutaneous (milk) vein at this site may produce a very large, elongated, practically painless swelling. A previous hæmatoma in this region may have left an area of fibrosis.

The ribs may be inspected for old or existing fractures and the abdominal wall examined, especially with a view to the presence of ventral or umbilical herniæ.

The cow will be walked to determine the presence or absence of lameness, and her feet will receive careful attention. Any unnatural separation or spreading of the claws will be noted, and especial attention paid to the inter-digital space, as well as to the length of the toes. Turning-up and overgrowth of their extremities should be recorded, as well as any indication of foot-soreness, excessive wear of the soles, or laminitis.

The udder and teats of the dairy cow must be inspected very carefully. The volume of the udder and the relative size of the four quarters must be scrutinised with great care, first by observation from several angles and then by palpation of each separate quarter. The hind quarters and the hind teats, especially in a cow which has borne several calves, will probably be slightly larger than the fore quarters, and this is perfectly normal. The disparity in the size of the teats should not be very marked, however, and the existence (especially in Guernseys) of immense "bottle teats" should be recorded. These are exceptionally large, very thin-walled teats which fill up with milk. Not rarely they possess a small or indurated orifice which is partially responsible for the condition, although bottle teats may be a hereditary feature in some strains of cattle. Any leakage from teats will be observed. It is not uncommon for teats which are "bursting" as the result of a heavy lactation in an over-stocked cow to emit small streams of milk, but a teat attached to a quarter apparently not overfilled with milk should never leak. A teat which leaks is sometimes attached to a comparatively *small* quarter which tends either to develop a mastitis or to become prematurely "dry", and it may sometimes carry an imperfectly healed sphincter.

The surface of the teats must be examined for abrasions, the marks of rubber bands, warts, cow pox, or other ulcerative conditions. The teat sphincter will be searched for the presence of black spot, for any scars suggestive of surgical interference, and its patency must be tested to discover whether the teat milks freely, whether any obstruction is present, or if the flow of milk is *too* free.

The teat canal will be palpated by rolling it between finger and thumb and noting any "peas" within the teat, fibroses, or calculi.

The surface, especially the hinder edge of each teat, must be examined for the presence of a teat fistula, and one should look between each fore and hind teat and at the rear of each hind teat either for existing supernumerary teats or for supernumerary teats which have been removed and may still possess an aperture through which some milk may be squeezed.

Supernumerary teats are almost invariably attached to a supernumerary quarter or milk gland, and a teat which has been removed and its aperture sealed may still be connected with a small swelling, rather superficially placed upon a quarter or between two quarters. This may represent a secreting glandular structure which may at any time develop a mastitis. These supranumerary glands are more prominent in newly calved cows and tend to "dry off" after a week or two and so disappear until the next lactation.

Each teat must now be milked separately into a stripping cup and particular attention paid to the foremilk and the strippings to determine whether clots are present. One should then have all four quarters milked out completely and the volume of milk from each quarter recorded. It will be mentioned in the certificate whether the calf was with the cow or if it had been removed prior to the examination. When all four quarters are empty they will again be checked for size, whether the two fore quarters and the two hind quarters exactly match or whether any quarter appears somewhat atrophied. One will note whether an apparent atrophy corresponds, or not, with a comparable reduction in the volume of milk it has yielded.

Each quarter is now very gently and carefully palpated in order to discover any evidence of swelling, atrophy, or fibrous induration. The supra-mammary glands are also examined and their size noted.

The limbs and joints will be inspected and, if necessary, palpated for bony enlargements or synovial distensions.

The body of the cow is "rocked" gently by pressure with the hand upon each pin-bone to determine whether there is any luxation of the lumbo-sacral articulations, which will be demonstrated by a knocking sound coming from the sacral region. The cow will be moved a few times either on a halter or free, and one will notice whether she travels in a straight line or if there is any sign of "rockiness" in her gait.

Any marked straightness of the hocks, grinding the teeth, paddling upon the toes of the hind feet, and an elevated tail head, with a tendency to stagger on the hind limbs, may raise doubts in a newly calved cow as to the existence of a calcium deficiency, with the possible onset of milk-fever.

In aged cows rheumatic, arthritic, and synovial conditions, particularly affecting the stifles, hip joints, and hocks, must be recognised.

The vulva must be examined for the presence of scars or indurations, which by causing puckering of its lips might permit the intake of air and fæces and so interfere with the animal's fertility.

One should also induce the cow to micturate by gently stroking the perineum immediately below the clitoris.

During micturition one notices the discharge of any

uterine fluids, the appearance of shreds or lengths of after-birth, and also any signs of hæmaturia.

If the calf is still with the cow it will be examined for size and development and any congenital defects; knuckling of the joints, rickets, atresia of the anus or vulva, umbilical hernia, cleft palate, and entropion being among the number. Any sign of diarrhœa will be sought for, and one will observe if the calf appears bright and eager to suck. The navel will be inspected. After the first few days this should be free from swelling, with a dry umbilical cord. It should have withered by the tenth day and should have disappeared at a fortnight.

THE BULL is submitted to a general examination in the same way as the cow, but whereas in the latter the greatest care is paid to the organs of lactation, in the bull the greatest attention is directed to a detailed examination of its genital organs.

The prepuce should be free from swelling. The hair at its extremity should be clean and free from signs of preputial discharge, and the hairs should not have been trimmed with scissors, as this encourages inturning of the scrotal skin, with resulting paraphimosis.

The penis may be palpated through the posterior portion of the prepuce and should be difficult to feel unless it is swollen or in any way misshapen ("broken penis"). If any doubt exists, the bull should be led out and "teased" with a cow in order that the extremity of the penis may be seen. Any distortion resulting from injury or hæmatoma should readily be observed. Many young bulls possess an infantile penis which fails to develop normally. There may also be a constricted preputial orifice, or warty growths may be present upon some portion of it which prevent its extrusion. In some young bulls failure to produce an erection may be due to a fibrosis of the retractor penis muscle, or this muscle may be short or almost entirely lacking.

The scrotum and testicles require a detailed examination.

Both testicles must have completely descended until they have reached the scrotal floor, and the two testicles with their epididymes and attached cords should fill the scrotum. There should be only a very slight difference in the relative size of the two testicles, the left is normally often a very little larger than the right.

A bull must never be passed as sound unless the two testicles lie completely parallel with each other. A hypoplastic testicle, one which is considerably smaller than its fellow, may lie vertically in the scrotum, but quite often it is inclined at an angle, so that although it is suspended from above by the spermatic cord the lower extremity is not in contact with the floor of the scrotum, but appears to be attached at one side of it, at some distance from its floor.

The epididymis should be distinctly palpable at the upper end of the testicle, and the two, one on either side, should be of equal size, without swelling or hardening due to fibrosis. Epididymitis is a not uncommon cause of infertility.

The two testicles should be firm to the touch, but should present no appearance of undue hardness owing to fibrous deposition, nor should they be abnormally large or heavy so that they distend the scrotum and cause it to hang unduly low to the ground. When the scrotum is grasped in the hand the scrotal walls and the cremasters should afford some evidence of contraction.

A testicle, or two testicles, affected with orchitis may or may not be painful according to the cause of the condition, but they are large, heavy, and usually adherent to the scrotum. Normally, if the testicles are raised by the left hand in the direction of the inguinal ring the loose skin of the scrotum, held in the right hand, can be pulled downwards, and when liberated the skin will return to its normal position. When orchitis is present this cannot usually be done, as inflammatory adhesions will have developed.

Ectopic testicles are by no means uncommonly encountered. They are usually smaller than normal testicles and possess shorter spermatic cords. The lower extremity of the testicle may partly protrude through the external inguinal ring, while in an occasional instance it may have left the canal and be contained beneath the skin of the abdominal wall in front of the scrotum. Needless to say, a bull showing any of the conditions recorded must be declared to be unsound.

Hernia within the scrotum is not very common in the bull, although it is so frequently encountered in the ram, but umbilical hernia is becoming a quite common condition, and as it is also hereditary, an animal possessing this defect must be rejected.

In adult and old bulls it is wise to examine the nostrils to make sure that they have not been torn through by the ring and ensure that their condition enables a bull to be led on a ring inserted into the nostrils with some degree of safety.

In adult bulls, too, the state of the feet is important, whether they are overgrown, sore, or laminitic. Any bull is only as good as his feet will permit him to be. The spine is another weak spot in many bulls, but it is not a part upon which it is always easy to express an opinion. The bull must be led out in order to judge whether it is sound, slightly lame, or sufficiently lame to interfere with its usefulness. It has been said that a bull with a sprained back or damaged spine turns around "all of a piece", which implies that it carries its back rigidly without lateral flexion. Arthritic hocks, stifles, or fetlocks will often cause a bull to refuse to serve, and it has been recorded that the presence of a traumatic reticulitis may have a similar effect.

Chapter Four

THE EXAMINATION OF SHEEP, GOATS, AND PIGS

The Examination of Sheep

Lambs are seldom sold alive before weaning age, but when examining a flock of ewes and lambs one must be on the look-out for various disease conditions such as swayback, "daft lambs", arthritis or joint ill, navel infections, rickets, bowel diseases, imperforate anus, the condition known as "double scalp", entropion, cleft palate, and even in lambs only a few weeks old one may encounter lameness arising from foot rot, as well as contagious pustular dermatitis ("orf"). These are only a few of the more common conditions which affect young sheep and lambs.

In adult sheep in general, one must pay attention to the condition of the fleece, note whether there are signs of "strike" (flyblow), lice, or other parasites. Observe also whether the fleece is loose and whether it pulls away easily in tufts or if it comes out in handfuls, with signs of irritation characterised by rubbing against posts and fences. Be on guard against the possibility of sheep scab, but venture no opinion unless the diagnosis is confirmed microscopically.

Neither Aujesky's disease, or scrapie, are likely to be encountered in sheep offered for sale privately, although in flocks put up by auction sale one may sometimes detect its existence.

The feet, in both lambs and ewes, may be affected with footrot or with an infection of the biflex canal which opens on to the midline of the digit, $\frac{1}{4}$ in. above the entrance to the interdigital space, in front of the pastern. This is absent in the goat.

In lactating ewes the udder requires very careful examination for evidence of mastitis, or one dry side, also for obstruction of the teat ducts. Shearing wounds may be important, as they harbour maggots and may also serve as an entrance for tetanus bacilli. The same risk is also present in lambs which have within the last fortnight been "tailed" or castrated. Castration by elastic ring is equally likely to be followed by tetanus.

Rams are quite frequently presented for examination.

The areas requiring special care in this respect are the skull, the mouth, and the genital organs.

The skull in a ram freshly introduced on a hillside or even into a small flock may become bruised by butting. It then swells and may become infected with *Clostridium œdematiens*, and unless treatment is promptly initiated the ram will in all probability die.

Rams which have been sent to a new owner by rail may produce the initial bruising by attacks upon the wall or door of the wagon carrying it.

The mouth requires examination for broken or missing incisors as well as for the presence of an overshot or undershot jaw. The same precautions should be taken as when examining the mouths of cattle, and the meeting of the incisor teeth with the dental pad must be inspected. Dental abnormalities dependent upon differences in the relative lengths of the mandible and maxilla may be transmitted by breeding stock.

The scrotum and testicles of the ram should be submitted

to examination on the same lines as those described in the bull, and a very careful inspection should be made in the ram for the existence of a scrotal hernia, now very common in certain breeds of sheep. It is a hereditary condition, and as otherwise valuable lambs are commonly submitted to operation for the relief of the hernia, the condition is likely to become even more common in the future.

The penis should be examined. Withdrawal from the prepuce is easier in the ram than in the bull. One must make certain that the vermiform appendix at the extremity of the penis is intact. It is sometimes removed by dishonest breeders in the belief that rams thus treated become infertile. Although there is little reason to credit this theory, the absence of the vermiform appendix must be considered an unsoundness.

In the ewe one must pay the same attention to the two sides of the udder as one does to the quarters of the cow. In the ewe, mastitis and loss of a half of the udder is very common. Teats also become damaged and may become occluded.

The Examination of the Goat

Generally speaking, what has been said about sheep applies to the goat, but the latter is peculiar on account of the numerous stages of intersexuality exhibited. In the female goat, especially, does this condition manifest itself, sometimes mainly by behaviour, but almost invariably also by changes in the clitoris and vulva. The vulva is often small and appears to possess either no vagina or a very constricted passage. The clitoris becomes somewhat enlarged and may exhibit a small, erect, horn-like protuberance, which is in reality an undeveloped penis. Others are confirmed nymphomaniacs and demonstrate their failing continuously in vocal fashion.

Changes may occur in the testicles, epididymes, and spermatic cords of male goats, but more generally they do not develop all the male characteristics (including the goaty aroma), and either show no inclination to serve or if they do so are usually infertile.

Goats suffer from ordinary foot rot as do sheep, but lacking a biflex canal, they do not suffer, as sheep do, from lameness arising from inflammation of the coronary region associated with this structure.

The Examination of the Pig

Young pigs to be offered for sale privately, or by auction, may be examined for a variety of conditions:

(1) Any state of disease or ill-health characterised by diarrhœa, loss of appetite, skin rashes, either urticarial or due to swine erysipelas (diamonds), avitaminosis, parasitic infestation, or ringworm. Skin or bowel œdema, with œdema of the eyelids and face; cough; necrosis of ear or tail; convulsions; lameness, especially when associated with arthritic conditions; joint ill; navel ill; and many other states of ill-health.

(2) Congenital abnormalities. These are also very numerous in their variety, and by no means uncommon in their appearance. They include: hairlessness and sometimes a reversal of the hair direction; cleft palate and nasal deformities, atrophic rhinitis, bilobed and dwarfed ears; deformed limbs and kinky tail; umbilical and scrotal herniæ; atresia of the anus and vulva; hermaphroditism or more commonly some degree of intersexuality; rachitic tendencies, spastic or bowed limbs; undershot and overshot jaws; ocular conditions, including absence of the eyeball (anophthalmia, microphthalmia), strabismus, and cataract.

All the pigs of a litter may not show a similar degree of development or growth rate.

(3) The acquired defects of pigs include those caused by bites and injuries, such as tearing of the ears, skin and lips of the vulva, hæmatoma and abscess formation. Abscesses are found in a considerable proportion of pigs slaughtered in the

abbattoir. One may also include among acquired defects verrucose endocarditis, which is a very common condition in pigs, and one which may never be observed unless it causes serious circulatory trouble. In some degree it may be present in any boar or sow, and may ultimately prove to be a cause of premature death. It can frequently be detected by auscultation applied over the triceps and ribs. It results usually from an attack of swine erysipelas which may have been so mild that it escaped notice.

Parasitic infestations, helminthiasis, and chronic skin irritations, as well as cough, cause loss of flesh or failure to grow at a normal rate and are forms of unsoundness.

Rickets may appear at an early age or at a later stage of growth; lameness from arthritis caused by swine erysipelas infection or by Glasser's disease.*

In adult sows mastitis is frequent; nipples become damaged by the teeth of suckling piglets; sometimes the nipples are few in number, irregularly spaced, or the nipples themselves may be inverted so that the piglets suck milk through them only with difficulty.

In gilts, defects of the genital organs and intersexuality are by no means uncommon. Tearing or fibrosis of the vulva may occur from bites, wounds occurring during parturition, or as a result of hæmatoma.

In boars one will look for any evidence of intersexuality, the presence of a vulva and testicles contained in a scrotum, both present in the same animal—also for underdeveloped testicles—and particularly for scrotal hernia in an otherwise normal boar. This is a defect commonly encountered in young pigs, although they are seldom permitted to mature unless the defect has gone unnoticed.

Atrophic rhinitis and eye defects must also be carefully sought after in the animal intended for breeding.

* See B.V.A. Handbook, *The Husbandry and Diseases of Pigs*, Section V, pp. 77–8.

Chapter Five

THE EXAMINATION OF THE DOG

In the case of the dog there are several meanings of the word "soundness". The veterinary meaning remains as ever, and the practising veterinary surgeon will regard a dog as being sound if it is not lame, and if it possesses no visible defect which is likely to interfere with its usefulness. Here, again, we have to consider what constitutes usefulness. A dog may be used as a guard dog, a gundog, to be employed for herding or driving sheep or cattle, for hunting or for going underground, or it may be required simply as a companion or pet, or, in the case of registered, pedigree animals, for showing and breeding. Obviously a dog may be quite capable of being a good house dog when it could not withstand the stress of a day's hunting or working cover with a man and a gun.

Condition plays a large part in this case. Even the house dog, if exercised regularly and more carefully fed, might become a great deal more athletic.

The question therefore arises: "Is a dog to be adjudged sound for a particular purpose, or is soundness to be based on purely physical grounds, irrespective of the purpose for which the dog is required?" The answer appears to be that in examining a dog for purchase, one should set a high standard of bodily soundness, as well as of physical fitness, without regard to the possible future environment of the animal, or the use to which it is to be put.

In this case we are expressing the veterinary aspect. As opposed to this we have that of the fancier, exhibitor, or show-judge, who regards unsoundness as some feature of conformation, gait, or occasionally even of temperament, which prevents the animal being a perfect specimen of its breed. Characteristics which would be regarded as constituting soundness in a Pekingese or Scottish Terrier would be regarded as rank unsoundness in a Greyhound or Alsatian.

Of the three hundred breeds of dog scheduled, the animals comprising at least one hundred and fifty of these breeds are the victims of acromegaly or achondroplasia, and judged as individuals are congenitally unsound. The result is that both veterinary surgeon and show-judge have to accept each animal as a member of a particular variety, complete with the deformities associated with that variety, and to declare the animal sound or unsound according to whether it is free from or possesses additional physical defects which render it even more of a cripple than the average specimen of its own particular breed.

In the show-ring a terrier with one or both forelimbs the very least bit out of the perpendicular, would be considered unsound, but the veterinary surgeon could not condemn it, as nothing exists which would interfere with the usefulness of the animal outside the show-ring. If the limbs were positively mis-shapen or rickety, then the dog would be unsound in the veterinary sense.

In the same way the show-dog with slack pasterns, a tail which was carried high when the standard decreed that it should be carried low, or vice versa, would be unsound in the eyes of the fancier, but not in those of the veterinary surgeon. The latter might prefer a whippet with a well-laid-back shoulder, sloping withers, and a long neck, and while the show judge would condemn a specimen with upright shoulders and a short neck as unsound, the veterinary surgeon might not be able to do so, because his definition of unsoundness differs from that of the fancier.

Both the veterinary surgeon and the show judge will agree that a dog which is badly out at elbows, is knock-kneed, cow-hocked, or possesses an undershot or overshot jaw is unsound.

They will also be in agreement since 1st January 1959, that a dog in which only one testicle is present in the scrotum is unsound, and the veterinary surgeon examining dogs prior to their being judged at a show will reject any which are not entire, i.e., which have not two testicles descended and in the scrotum. Dogs which have been treated for cryptorchidism or monorchidism on veterinary advice are, similarly, not eligible to be shown, and must be rejected by the veterinary examiners. The purpose of the new Show Regulations, which have the full support of the B.V.A., is to prevent the exhibition of dogs which are not entire, with the intention that the use of such dogs at stud will decrease.

The differences between the professional view of soundness and that accepted by the fancier has been stressed in order that the veterinary surgeon asked by a client living in some remote part of the country or abroad to examine a dog, will realise that there are two ordinarily accepted standards of soundness and unsoundness, and it is always well to know exactly which a client has in mind.

The majority of veterinary examinations of dogs carried out in this country are concerned mainly with the freedom of the subject from infectious disease or from the risk of having been in contact with an infected dog. No veterinary surgeon is able to guarantee that a dog is not in the incubation period of a disease, and after making a careful examination of the nose, eyes, mucous membranes, temperature, pulse, and respiration, and finding nothing amiss, the only statement he can honestly make in his certificate is that *at the time of his examination* he was unable to detect any evidence of a febrile disease. He may do this with a greater degree of confidence if he knows that the dog has been previously injected with an accepted vaccine against distemper and Leptospirosis, and immunised, as far as possible, against Rubarth's disease.

Routine Examination of the Dog

Before the dog is handled it is well to see it in action upon the ground. It should be led away from the examiner and back again at walking pace, then trotted slowly alongside its handler. In this way any sign of lameness will be detected. One will also notice whether the dog walks a straight line or rolls behind from side to side, whether it "plaits" (puts the hind foot in the imprint made by the forefoot, a fault in action), whether it flexes all its joints so that from behind the pads become visible when each foot is lifted. It will also be observed whether the dog "hops" occasionally on one hind limb with the opposite foot held off the ground momentarily (a sign of patellar subluxation), and also whether the trochanters of the femur appear unduly prominent (muscular atrophy) and appear to "wobble" as the dog walks (a sign of hip dysplasia).

Intermittent lameness in the hind limb is very frequent from patellar causes in the short-limbed dogs (Cairns, Sealyhams, West Highlands, and Scottish Terriers), while hip dysplasia, although now seen in numerous breeds, is more commonly encountered in Bulldogs, Bostons, Alsatians, and is becoming increasingly common in Labradors. It is very common, and has been so for many years, in the smaller toy breeds.

A tendency to sit, whenever brought to a halt, may have been ingrained by teaching, but it is also a common symptom of hip dysplasia.

Stifle lameness may be associated with growth stages in young dogs, and the patella sometimes retains its position more satisfactorily when the femur and tibia have attained their adult size relation, but in Cairns, particularly, the "hopping" action may persist throughout life.

In greyhounds hind-limb lameness may be due to the usual causes, but hock injuries (scaphoid fracture and injuries to the os calcis), as well as digital fractures and periarticular fibrosis, are especially common.

The so-called Scottie cramp must be looked for in Scottish Terriers, and is emphasised if the dog is excited in play, then taken for a fast run. The lameness comes on gradually, with a shuffling action of the limbs, and if the exercise is persisted in the dog may eventually fall upon its side and for several minutes, or longer, it will be unable to regain its footing. This condition, very common a few years ago, is fast disappearing.

The dog, returning towards the examiner, may show forelimb lameness. The shoulder joint or elbow may be involved, and injuries to the condyles of the humerus or head of the radius and ulna may be responsible. The greatest case of lameness in the fore limbs lies in the feet. Interdigital cysts, overgrown nails, foreign bodies, eczema, cracks in the pads, and infection and loosening of the nails are common conditions. In young dogs and puppies bone conditions, including rickets, may be responsible. The crushed toes caused by treads must also be looked for, especially in the larger breeds. In greyhounds, toe injuries, fractured sesamoids, and pisiform bones must be recognised.

At the conclusion of the examination for gait, have the dog lifted on to a table. After making friends with the animal, raise its head gently, bending it slightly backwards upon the neck, then press down upon its lumbar region with the palm of the hand and see if either of these actions produce signs of pain. "Rheumatism" and disc abnormalities may often be brought to light in this way.

Now observe the respiration, count the pulse, auscultate the heart, and take the temperature. Although the temperature

I

is mentioned last, it is usually better taken first, as any degree of handling or excitement will temporarily raise the temperature by one or more degrees. Make a careful note at the time of your recordings.

The heart of the dog, especially if it be a large animal, is frequently somewhat intermittent, and this need not be considered abnormal in the absence of cardiac murmurs. If it causes any suspicion, have the dog trotted fast for a hundred yards and brought back and immediately re-examine the heart. In many cases with a more frequent heart beat the intermittency may disappear. Any adventitious sounds suggestive of a valvular lesion will be carefully noted.

Next, examine the whole skin surface, particularly that of the abdomen and axillæ for the presence of disease such as dermatitis, moist eczema, ringworm, mange, or other parasitic disease.

The ribs will be inspected and palpated for past or present fractures.

Next palpate the abdomen.

In the bitch one gently grasps it from beneath between fingers and thumb, feeling particularly for pyometra or pregnancy. Pregnancy is best detected at the twenty-second day, when fœtuses feel like a chain of beads, each approximating a marble in size with an easily appreciable space between each. After a month detection is more difficult owing to the accumulation of fluid around each fœtus and the disappearance of the space between each. At six weeks there is an abdominal fullness which may be confused with fatness or pyometra, but the presence of other signs may help to decide. One will also feel for any enlargement of the spleen which may be present, for neoplasms, and particularly for enlargement of the lymph nodes or the presence of stones or other foreign bodies in the intestine and for calculi in the bladder. Fæcoliths, especially in old dogs, must not be confused with foreign bodies.

In the male dog the scrotum will be very carefully examined to determine if both testicles are present and of normal size and if scrotal hernia is present. If only one can be felt, then the skin at either side of the prepuce, the flank and inner side of the thigh, should be palpated in search of an ectopic testicle. The penis will be exposed and examined for evidence of granuloma.

The anal region will be inspected for the presence of a fistula, furunculosis of the perianal tissues with the development of sinuses, anal adenoma (almost always in males only), and for the presence of distended anal glands.

The fact that a somewhat odorous fluid can be expelled from the anal orifices when the glands are squeezed through the perianal tissues is not evidence of abnormality unless the discharge is inspissated, or purulent and highly offensive.

Returning to the head, examine both ear flaps for hæmatoma or for fibrosis and puckering resulting from its previous presence.

Look deeply into the aural canal (without the use of an auroscope) for the presence of a black deposit which is probably the excrement of ear parasites, for ulceration of the inner aspect of the concha, or for any evidence that an aural resection has at some time been performed.

Lift the lip and look carefully at the incisor teeth, see whether they are all present, firm, healthily disposed and level. Note the colour of the gum itself, the degree of pinkness, press it with the tip of the finger, and note how long it takes to refill with blood and return to its normal colour. Note any unpleasant smell from the breath, either from pyorrhea or oral sepsis, and particularly notice a smell resembling urine, which may be present in cases of nephritis and uræmia. Open the mouth widely, inspect the cheek teeth and the tonsils, using the light of an electric torch.

Note the size and prominence of the tonsils, also the size and "feel" of the submaxillary and prescapular glands.

Look at the nose itself; observe any dryness or cracking and any sign of an excessive or purulent discharge.

Watch carefully for any sign of twitching of the temporal muscles, or of the jaw, or a limb, or other sign of chorea.

Examine the pads of the feet, note whether they are hardened, horny, dry, or cracked. Look carefully at and between each toe and also at the nails. Observe any overgrowth of the nails and of those of the dewclaws, also any enlargements of the joints of the toes or any sign of fractures of the phalanges, past or present.

The eyes should now be given attention. Look at the lids for entropion, ectropion, inturned or double rows of eyelashes. Notice any abnormality of the third eyelid, whether it partly covers the eye, or if the Harderian gland is protruding or enlarged.

Look at the conjunctiva and note any discharge from the eye. Make sure there is no sign of a dermoid growing from the margins of the sclera and conjunctiva. See if the eyes are wide open or if either shows ptosis (dropping of a lid) or blepharospasm (painful closure of the lids). Now study the surface of the cornea for evidence of keratitis. Note any cloudiness or definite opacity or any sign of a corneal ulcer. Take particular notice of any vascularity of the cornea.

Note any abnormal dilatation or contraction of the pupil. When dilatation is present one may see a greenish reflection from the tapetum when light shines in the eye. In Irish Setters, especially, be on the look-out for night blindness, in which this appearance is shown. It may occur in almost any breed of dog.

Close one eyelid for a few moments and on releasing it observe whether the pupil has dilated as it should. Conversely, let the eyes face a bright light and notice whether both pupils contract.

The consensual reflex is not marked in the dog, so that when one eye is closed the pupil of the open eye does not dilate, and in many cases contraction of the pupil occurs only in the pupil actually stimulated by light.

The ophthalmoscope may be employed to examine the surface of the cornea, as well as the depths of the eye, and also to determine whether or not cataract is present. As a rule this defect can be recognised by direct illumination, but the ophthalmoscope provides the surest method of diagnosis.

Coming to the fore limbs, examine the shoulders and elbows carefully, noting any loss of muscle over either scapula. Carefully flex each elbow in turn to its full extent to determine whether any soreness exists (as in an old condyle injury). Note the straightness or curvature of the radius and ulna and any enlargement of the knees. Notice any callosities on the sternum, elbows, or knees arising from lying on a hard floor.

The pasterns and feet vary considerably according to the animal's breed, its environment, and whether it has been exercised on hard roads, on soft ground, or not at all. The pasterns of any dog will become slack through lack of exercise, or if the animal is exercised in fields or in public grass parks. In the same way the feet become splayed and the toes lose their natural bunching and become extended. The nails grow long and tend to curl under the toes. The dew claws, particularly if they are present on the hind feet, grow round in circles and frequently bury their points in the flesh of the limb. In most of the terrier breeds and in greyhounds the toes should be bunched together (cat feet) and not splayed out (hare feet). In some of the larger galloping breeds hare feet, with a good deal of long hair growing from around and between the toes, are employed as brake and anti-skid devices.

In all galloping breeds examine the toes carefully for missing or "knocked-up" toes. Missing toes are probably produced by the amputation of knocked-up toes, which have been broken or damaged by tearing of their ligaments. They then become surrounded by fibrous tissue, remain painful and slow down the dog, especially on corners. There is usually lameness shown after a gallop, which improves with rest, only to recur at the next outing. Interdigital cysts may be found between the toes of the forefeet, but seldom in the hind feet. Broken and loosened toenails with septic coronitis involving their bases, are common not only in racing dogs but also in terriers which dig and "go to ground".

When examining the hind limb of the dog the pelvis must first be observed from every possible angle and the position of each tuber coxæ ascertained and compared with its fellow. Crushing of the pelvis in a bitch may result in a diminished pelvic orifice, even after comparatively good healing has occurred.

As the result of injudicious breeding, the hip joint of the dog has become, during the past few years, the site of a great deal of deformity. The so-called hip dysplasia, in which there is a shrinking of the femoral head and a looseness of its articulation with the acetabulum, must now be sought in almost every breed. This, together with von Perthe's disease, may be encountered in quite young dogs (from four months) as well, of course, as in the adults.

The hip disease most common in dogs which have survived to old age is a rheumatoid arthritis. As hip dysplasia, excepting in toy breeds, is a condition which has only recently made itself very evident, it is likely that in future years it will also be commonly met with in the hips of old dogs which have been permitted to go through life with impaired hip joints. Quite a number of dogs may be found, and even recognised with some difficulty, which are affected with a chronic dislocation of the hip joint. In these dogs a dislocated hip, incurred possibly months or years previously, has either never been replaced, or the head of the femur has repeatedly slipped out of the acetabulum, with the result that fibrous tissue has been laid down with the formation of a false joint.

Such animals develop a compensatory gait which is not at all noticeable, in fact apparent recovery may occur to such an extent that a greyhound owning one of these false hip joints may occasionally course quite successfully and show little or no sign of lameness.

Although it is sufficient to describe a dog as being unsound in its hip joint without the need for a more precise diagnosis, this condition is mentioned, as it may easily be missed without an X-ray examination.

In the hind limb, too, old femoral fractures may sometimes be recognised by permanent callus formation. Here, again, there may be some shortening of the limb, but a compensatory action minimises lameness, and the defect may be hard to detect.

The stifle joint requires a very studied examination. Each stifle should be carefully flexed in turn and compared the one with the other. Any crepitation or grating will be noticed, as well as signs of pain. The inner aspect of the femoro-tibial articulation must be carefully palpated for signs of enlargement, usually painful, due to injury to the ligaments and displacement of the semilunar cartilages. When atrophy of the cartilage has occurred the femur and tibia can be gently drawn apart a little way by traction, and when liberated the bones will come again into apposition, accompanied by a knocking sound.

Subluxation of the patella can often be detected by alternately flexing and extending the stifle joint when the patella will be felt slipping over the edge of the medial trochlea. In this case a grating sound is heard.

Dogs are examined by a veterinary surgeon before the commencement of judging at the majority of dog shows, and at all open shows under Kennel Club rules.

The veterinary surgeon is usually stationed near the entrance, or in fine summer weather even outside it when shows are held in marquees in fields. He should provide himself with a suitable white overall coat and rubber gloves, while some arrangement must be made by which he may dip his gloved hands in disinfectant and dry them between handling one dog and the next.

Normally, he should do little handling but should ask the attendant in charge of the dog to open its mouth, remove its rugs, and exhibit the various parts of its body.

It will usually be necessary for him to palpate the scrotum in every case in which it is not obvious to the eye that both testicles are present within it.

He will take the temperature in all suspicious cases, but it is not usual to do so in the case of each exhibit.

The best appliance is made up of three benches, one raised on boxes or a table, and one bench at either end, inclined, so that the dog walks up one end, stands on the table to be examined, and walks down the other.

It is wise to write, or ask a steward to write down the number of each dog as it is examined, and to check up on absentees, or on dogs which have been benched without examination.

If the veterinary surgeon finds a dog which he feels should be rejected, he should write on a slip of paper the number and breed of the dog and the cause of rejection and hand it to the steward to be given immediately to the show secretary.

The causes of rejection will be any sign of a febrile disease such as distemper, allowance of $1°-1\frac{1}{2}°$ F. being made for excitement caused by the environment; cryptorchidism or the ectopic testicle; any skin disease of a parasitic and contagious nature. Other conditions may be hysteria, blindness, complete deafness, acute catarrhal conditions, painful ear disease, vomiting, or diarrhœa.

Allowance must always be made, especially in young dogs, for the possible effects of travel sickness. Although, at present, it is not the concern of the veterinary surgeon, some dogs arrive at a show so completely "doped" with remedies against this condition that they are hardly fit to enter the ring. Other dogs may be showing the effect of overdosing with a "tranquilliser". The Kennel Club has now ruled that the use of a tranquilliser is "calculated to deceive" and is therefore undesirable.

Bitches in season should always be pointed out to the steward. Where the particular show regulations do not bar them, some arrangement will usually be made to bench them away from male exhibits.

Chapter Six

EXAMINATION OF THE GREYHOUND

By J. K. BATEMAN, B.Sc., M.R.C.V.S., Veterinary Surgeon
to the Greyhound Racing Association, Ltd.

THE examination of the greyhound for soundness can be
properly undertaken only if the examiner is aware of the
physical defects and the various injuries and lamenesses to
which the greyhound is subject. It is wise to have the dog
standing erect on a level surface and for the examiner to
make a preliminary survey by quietly walking round the dog,
viewing him from various angles.

The animal under review must be free from defect or deformity, and must be sound in eye, wind, and limb. The
examiner should start by examining the head then the chest,
hips, and sexual organs, then the forelimbs, left limb first,
and finally the hind limbs.

The anatomical features to be examined and physical defects to be looked for and avoided, are as follows:

(1) Eyes. The greyhound must have good sight and must
not suffer from corneal opacity or cataract, both of which are
rare. A not uncommon condition, however, is that which is
probably an affection of the optic nerve and in which the
greyhound's eyes are permanently dilated, the pupils failing

to react to light. This prevents the greyhound from seeing his quarry at close quarters or under lights, and is a serious unsoundness.

(2) Ears. Deafness has been seen particularly in white dogs. Test to sound.

(3) Mouth. There must be no jaw deformity, e.g., overshot mouth, which is an unsoundness in a hunting dog, and the mouth must be otherwise normal—examine the tonsils, which might be temporarily inflamed or enlarged.

(4) Chest. The chest should be auscultated and percussed. Pleurisy is sometimes present, other chest conditions being rare. The heart beat and pulse should be steady and regular. Irregularities, though not uncommon, should never be disregarded. Respiration is slow in the healthy, unexcited dog. Emphysema is rare.

(5) The hips. It is fairly common to see a greyhound with one hip down—more often the right than the left. Such a condition does not appear to affect the running of the animal. It probably occurs at birth, and only serious deformities are regarded as unsoundnesses, though they must be mentioned in any report.

(6) The tail. For track-racing purposes a dog with only half a tail would not be classed as unsound. Such an animal would be unlikely to be acceptable as sound on the coursing field, where turning at speed is more frequent and change of direction is common.

(7) Testicles. A male greyhound may have two testicles, one testicle, or none. The two latter conditions are hereditary, and although such greyhounds may race well and one possessing only one testicle within the scrotum may prove fertile, the condition is definitely an unsoundness in either case.

The Forelimbs

(*a*) The pads. Each foot must have four good top pads and a sound fleshy sole pad—all free from corns.

(*b*) Nail roots. The nail roots or quicks should be soft and resilient and free from cracks and suppuration. Each joint of every toe must be capable of being freely flexed and extended.

(*c*) Toe joints. Enlargement of the joints denotes repair to partial dislocation, new or old, with consequent fixation, in greater or lesser degree with tendency to lameness.

(*d*) Each Metacarpal–phalangeal joint must be free from enlargement, which may mean a previous torn collateral ligament or a fractured sesamoid.

(*e*) The metacarpal bones, being subject to fracture in the young, must be examined and found free from ossification.

(*f*) Dewclaws should be present. Their absence does not denote unsoundness.

(*g*) The Carpus must be capable of being freely flexed and should be able to withstand sufficient gentle pressure to allow the sole pad to approximate the skin over the flexor muscles. In racing greyhounds, fracture of the right pisiform bone is common. Flexion of the carpus in such a case evinces pain.

(*h*) The forearm is sometimes fractured—examine for exostosis.

(*i*) The left elbow must have no lateral exostosis on the head of radius.

The upper limb is subject to much stress and injury. Examine carefully both legs for depressions due to muscle tearing or formation of knots of fibrous tissue. Look for any muscle wasting over the scapula due to nerve injury, Extend and flex each shoulder joint carefully. Run the hands down the anterior border of the scapula for evidence of pain on the course of the suprascapular nerve.

The Hind Limbs

In the pes areas are subject to similar injury as in the fore-limbs.

Both hocks must be free from exostosis, particular care being given to the right scaphoid area. Enlargement constitutes unsoundness. Examine the medial surface of the left tibia for exostosis or other deformity (track leg). Examine the left stifle for evidence of injury due to collision with the inner (track) fence when racing.

Carefully palpate the muscle area behind each stifle joint for evidence of former muscle tearing and deposition of fibrous tissue. The presence of fibrous tissue "knots" in the body of any muscle, wherever situated, constitutes an unsoundness, since the site is vulnerable and liable to further injury at work.

Movement

Have the dog first walked then trotted and check on any departure from normal, always bearing in mind that one cannot expect to detect a muscle injury on observation alone, for many greyhounds suffering from torn muscles will trot level but are unable to extend themselves at a gallop.

Finally, before any deal is completed in the case of a valuable greyhound, see the dog after a hare on a track, although, apart from physical unsoundness, the performance of the dog is not the responsibility of the veterinary surgeon.

Chapter Seven

EXAMINATION OF THE CAT

By Margaret A. W. Bentley, M.R.C.V.S.

The examination of the cat for soundness follows closely that
of the dog, and each breed of cat should conform to the
general standards established for its breed as well as being in
sound physical condition if it is to be considered wholly
sound.

A cat is best examined on a table under a good light, and
on being taken out of its basket may be stroked gently and
picked up to allow it to get used to its surroundings. This
also tells one whether the cat is too fat, too thin, or if it is a
nervous animal. Viciousness may be found in the cat as in
other animals, and a cat which cannot be handled by the
judges need not be judged at shows.

The temperature should be taken early in the examination,
allowing a rise of 1 or 2 degrees for fright.

The detailed examination is begun at the head. Look at
the eyes, noting their reaction to light, and carefully examining the lids for distichiasis, usually found at the inner canthus
and on the upper eyelid; cats with distichiasis are unsound,
and should not be bred from. Entropion is frequently found
in the flat-faced varieties of cat, accompanied by trichiasis,
with persistent keratitis and epiphora.

"Tear stains" or staining of the skin of the face at the inner canthus would indicate obstruction of the naso-lacrimal ducts, due to inflammation of the ducts from conjunctivitis, or even the absence of the ducts. If a few drops of fluorescin are instilled into the conjunctival sac it will be seen to run down the face instead of appearing at the nasal orifice. This dye will also reveal any corneal ulceration that may have been produced by friction of the eyelashes in trichiasis or distichiasis.

Occasionally litters of kittens are seen with congenital absence of part or all of the tarsal plate in the upper eyelid. Any lashes present or even the hairs of the face will be in continual contact with the cornea causing a persistent blepharospasm and epiphora.

The presence of a purulent conjunctivitis in an adult cat, especially if found with a purulent coryza, may be considered suspicious of early infection with one of the varieties of cat influenza.

The protrusion of the membrana nictitans indicates a general loss of condition, and signs of general illness should be carefully sought. It is due to the absorption of the post-orbital fat, and recession of the eyeball, and is found during a heavy moult or in stud cats at the end of a mating season.

Microphthalmos is easily detected if unilateral, but may not be noticed if it is bilateral, unless accompanied by other congenital defects, such as nystagmus or strabismus. Strabismus is often seen in the Siamese cat, but is considered a fault to be eliminated from the breed, show standards requiring the eyes to be "clear, bright, decidedly blue, with an oriental shape, slanting towards the nose but no tendency to squint".

Examine the nose and lips for "rodent ulcers", and varying degrees of hare lip, particularly in the flat-faced breeds. Open the mouth and look at the teeth, noting any malposition of the canine teeth. The gums should be pink and glistening, there should be no staining of the teeth, offensive breath, or evidence of gingivitis, such as bleeding gums or loosened teeth. The tongue should be free from ulcers, and if possible the tongue should be raised to look for sub-lingual ranulas.

Any female cat wanted for breeding should be free from conjunctivitis and coryza, or any other evidence of catarrh, such as noisy breathing, or dyspnœa if the mouth is held closed for a few moments. Such an animal should be considered unsound for breeding, as she is probably a carrier of cat influenza and will infect her kittens by licking them.

The ears should be examined next. Bare areas of skin in front of the ear may indicate infestation of the auditory meatus with *Otodectes otodectes*. Similarly, patches of desquamated skin with scab formation behind the ears showing that the cat has been scratching at them should lead one to suspect parasitic infestation of the ears. Heavy infestations of *Otodectes* may easily be seen with the naked eye, the small cream-coloured mites move rapidly among the wax in the ear canal and even on the skin of the head in front of the ear. Less severe parasitism will require the use of an auroscope, and by the same means the deeper parts of the auditory meatus can be searched for the granulomatous swellings sometimes found at the base of the vertical conchal canal, and which cause persistent head shaking or even force the cat to carry the head dropped on one side. These granulomatous swellings are nearly always present if the canal contains a creamy pus with a foul necrotic odour. The conchal cartilage should be felt for hæmatoma or for the contraction of the cartilage which follows the resolution of a hæmatoma.

The examination of the skin of a cat is of prime importance. The coat should be shining, and in the long-haired varieties should be thick in texture and free from matting. The skin should be thin, supple, and free from scurf.

The hair and skin should be examined first with the fingers, and then the hair may be parted with a fine comb to reveal any scurf, fleas, lice, or nits present.

Ringworm is by far the most difficult of all skin complaints to diagnose in the cat, and since it is the most contagious, it is very necessary to be thorough in the search, particularly in long-haired cats. Ringworm is rapidly contracted by all in contact, including humans, and each member of a household may be infected from a recently purchased kitten without the latter showing any obvious lesions. Such a kitten may be the cause of litigation, and if this is probable it would be wise to have laboratory confirmation of the diagnosis.

Infection with *Microsporon felineum* or *Trichophyton felineum* is usually confined to young cats or kittens of the long-haired variety, but it can, of course, be found in the short-haired breeds that have been in contact with an infected cat at a dealer's. The lesions may show up as small circles of slightly thickened skin with whitish epithelial scales lying among broken hairs. Only very rarely do they appear as obvious rings of skin denuded of hair. These small circles, often only a few millimetres in diameter, are found on the face, head, neck, ears, and forequarters; and if such areas are discovered with epithelial scales, specimens of the suspected and broken hairs should be examined under a Wood's lamp if available, or preferably under a microscope. If suspected hairs are touched with a drop of chloroform they are said to fluoresce, or shine like hoar frost; this may arouse one's suspicions but is not definite proof of infection.

Another form of ringworm more rarely seen is *Favus* or "honey comb" ringworm. It is caused by *Achorion schonleinii*, and the lesions will usually be found at the base of the claw. If the retractile claw is withdrawn the surrounding skin will appear swollen with yellowish crater-like crusts. Occasionally these typical craters will be found on the nose, face, and forelegs. The cat is infected from mice, and will in

K

turn infect other animals and man, but the spread is less rapid than in the other two varieties, and is more inclined to die out before being passed on to in-contacts. Microscopic examination will enable distinction to be made between the varieties.

Notoedric mange or "head mange" is found only rarely, and shows itself as a thickening and corrugation of the skin of the forehead, face, and neck, with loss of hair from the affected skin, and numerous vesicles and scabs. As *notoedres* is a member of the sarcoptic mange family, there is invariably an intense pruritis, and evidence of self-inflicted damage to the skin by the cat's attempts to gain relief from the irritation. Patient search of skin scrapings should enable one to find the parasite, and to distinguish between this condition and an eczematous skin.

Demodectic mange is not known in the cat.

Heavy infestations with fleas or lice should really be classed as unsoundness, being a reflection on the hygiene of the breeder or fancier; and also because they are rapidly transmitted to all other animals on the premises and cause unthriftiness, anæmia, and carry bowel parasites.

Infestation with *Cheyletiella parasitorvax* might very rarely be found in roaming country cats who hunt rabbits. This parasite resembles the harvester, and is free living on the skin. It can readily be seen with the naked eye as rapidly moving whitish mites, about the size of harvesters, on any part of the body. They are usually present in large numbers, and can be caught in a fine tooth comb. They cause an acute irritation, and will live on humans, causing an irritant rash on the trunk.

The so-called "miliary eczema" should be distinguished from notoedric mange. Eczema is most frequently found in the overweight neuter, as a pin-point papular rash widely spread over the body, and often accompanied by a flea infestation. In long-standing cases the lesions coalesce into large, moist, ulcerated plaques, with loss of hair from licking, and considerable scab formation. The most usual sites are the neck, back, and thighs.

The examination of the gait of the cat is not as easy or as important as in the dog. If the cat can be induced to walk, abnormalities due to previous pelvic fracture, or the circling gait from cerebellar imbalance will be detected.

By running the hand down the spine kyphosis and lordosis may be found. This "Switchback" spine is seen in the Siamese and related breeds, often associated with rachitis, or osteogenesis imperfecta. Luxation and even fracture of one or more vertebræ is a frequent occurrence in such spines, with a resultant permanent paraplegia. Such affected animals are unsound for show and breeding.

The pelvis of a female cat should be examined for healed fractures that might predispose to dystocia. The tail should likewise be examined for old fractures, particularly near the base; callus formation here may lead to staining and excoriation of the skin from urine or fæces. The tail of the Siamese may have a kink at the tip only.

The feet should be looked at for ingrowing claws, luxated digits, and polydactylism; the latter is a hereditary feature.

The abdomen should now be palpated, feeling for fœtuses, contracted kidneys, enlarged mesenteric glands or liver. If the bladder feels full it may be emptied manually through the abdominal wall, and the urine voided examined for albumen, blood, cell casts, or gravel deposits. A neutered male cat with a full bladder, and with the penis extruded, is suspicious of urethral obstruction.

The entire male should have the scrotum palpated to see that there are two testicles present. Absence of testicles in a male cat whose urine has the odour of an entire male would indicate retention of one or both testicles within the abdomen or at the inguinal ring.

The perivulval hair of the female neuter will be stained

with urine if the animal has the incontinence occasionally encountered after sterilisation.

The peri-anal hairs and skin of all cats should be free from adhering fæces or fæcal staining. In young cats, particularly, any evidence of this staining would merit the examination of a fæces specimen for parasitic ova or coccidial oocysts.

Umbilical hernia, and ventral hernia will be discovered during the palpation of the abdomen; both are hereditary and although less common than in the dog, cats showing them should not be used for breeding. The large fat pouches in the inguinal region of the neuter should not be mistaken for hernia.

The examination of the lungs and heart by auscultation is limited by the friction sounds of the hair on the stethoscope; however, gross pulmonary lesions can be detected, and any cat showing them would already have been noted as being unwell from its general appearance, behaviour, and posture. Radiological examination of the thoracic cavity would confirm the presence of tuberculosis, pleural effusion, or diaphragmatic hernia.

Although *Leptospira icterohæmorrhagiæ* and *Leptospira canicola* infection occur extremely rarely in the cat, it should be remembered that cats being exported to Australia must show a negative serological agglutination test for these two conditions before entry is permitted.

The Examination of Exhibits at Shows

The veterinary surgeon who undertakes the examination of cats and kittens at shows carries a heavy responsibility. Several hundred valuable and disease-prone animals will be congregated together for a considerable time, often after travelling long distances in unsuitable containers. Any kitten aged three calendar months and upwards may be shown, and litter classes are common, thus encouraging the transport of several kittens in one basket, often inadequately ventilated.

Allowances should be made for such kittens, who may be hot, nervous, and covered with excrement when first examined.

The veterinary surgeon should be provided with a steady table covered with some impervious material and large enough to hold both the cat and its container. Adequate light, and facilities for washing both the hands and the table are important. The provision of a capable steward can save both time and temper, and it is helpful to take along one's own lay assistant.

Each cat or kitten should be examined out of its basket, looking for skin parasites, evidence of powdering of the coat (which will disqualify in judging), and ringworm. A Wood's lamp is usually available at large shows. Any animal with discharging eyes, nose, or ulcerated tongue or any other suspicion of infection should have its temperature taken. If in the opinion of the veterinary surgeon any cat or kitten should not be allowed to enter or remain in the show, this opinion, stating the reason or reasons, should be given to the show secretary, in writing, together with the entrance number of the exhibit, as soon as possible.

Under Section 21 of the Governing Council of the Cat Fancy Regulations for Exhibition and Registration, "any exhibit disqualified from exhibition by the examining Veterinary Surgeon shall leave the hall immediately and if, in his opinion it is desirable, all other exhibits from the same Cattery and the owner thereof shall be debarred from attending the Show".

Under the same section of the regulations, it may be necessary to "examine any cat already admitted to the show pens against which an objection is brought on the grounds of its suffering from any contagious or infectious disease, or its having been prepared for exhibition in contravention of these rules made by the Council, and give in writing his duly signed opinion to the Show Secretary before the Show closes".

Doubtful cases for rejection should be allowed to remain in their baskets until all other entrants have been admitted. They may then be re-examined in consultation with another veterinary surgeon, if present, and if a slight rise in temperature was the sole cause for refusing entry, and if the second veterinary surgeon can see no other reason for refusing entry, and the temperature has not risen, they may be admitted.

Veterinary surgeons are instructed not to admit "cats obviously in kitten".

It is reasonable to assume that any cat which the examining veterinary surgeon does not consider to be in prime physical condition, either from heavy parasitic infestation or some other cause, is not in "Show" condition, and can be rejected for this reason alone, with advantage to the judges, breeders, visitors to the Show, and other exhibitors.

INDEX